To Simon
Happy Christmas 1986
All the Very Best
From
Mike

Tina

Tina

THE TINA TURNER STORY

BY RON WYNN

SIDGWICK & JACKSON
LONDON

First published in Great Britain in 1985
by Sidgwick and Jackson Limited

Originally published in the United States
of America by Macmillan Publishing Company,
a division of Macmillan, Inc.

Produced by Rapid Transcript, a Division of March Tenth, Inc.

Designed by Stanley S. Drate/Folio Graphics Co. Inc.

ISBN 0–283–99305–7

Printed in Great Britain by
The Garden City Press, Letchworth, Hertfordshire
for Sidgwick and Jackson Limited
1 Tavistock Chambers, Bloomsbury Way
London WC1A 2SG

Contents

This book is dedicated first and foremost to my family: my parents, James W. Wynn and Sammye Jefferson Wynn, who've always been supportive, regardless of their misgivings; my wife, Angela, for putting up with weird hours and records and books all over the place; my son, Khari, who's three going on forty; my sister, Ann Davis, for understanding a spaced-out brother; my aunt, Ruth Reed, for never losing faith; and my uncle, W. C. Reed, and grandmother, Annie Bell Hart, who knew it would happen but aren't here to see it.

It's also dedicated to people who've been inspirations all along the way: Trane, Ellington, Hendrix, James Brown, Little Walter Jacobs, Aretha, Miles, the Dells, the Temptations, Charlie Pride, the Rev. Martin Luther King, Jr., the Rev. Jesse Jackson, Langston Hughes, James Baldwin, and Ralph Ellison.

Acknowledgments

I'd like to acknowledge the following, without whose help this book would not be possible: Sandra Choron; Dave Marsh; Joanna Nicholson, who lent me both a typewriter and a library card; Kit Rachlis, for taking a chance seven years ago; Joe McEwen; Arthur Kempton; Milo Miles; Mike Freedberg; and Ken Ott and Kay Bourne, for sharing their passions for music with me and keeping mine stimulated and active.

BOB LEAFE

Introduction

Some twenty-four years ago Ike and Tina Turner scored their first hit single, "Fool in Love." Though its impact was confined to the black (R&B) charts, the song served as the introduction to the music universe of one Anna Mae Bullock, aka Tina Turner. At the time of the recording, Ike was the star; Tina just the rising newcomer. Ike was not only an accomplished bassist, guitarist, and pianist, but he'd already made a reputation for himself through his work as a talent scout for Modern Records in the fifties and through his connections with the Kings of Rhythm, who'd given the world one of the first definitive rock & roll records in 1951's "Rocket 88."

Almost a quarter-century later Ike resides quietly in St. Louis. He is known by most contemporary fans as a background character in some band Tina Turner once played in, or is scorned for his apparent mistreatment and domination of Tina during much of the time they were together, a chronicle whose depth shocked everyone but Tina's closest confidantes when they were made public. Today Tina's presence and stardom are legendary. But the Ike and Tina Turner Revue never remotely approached the level of media attention and public identification Tina currently enjoys. She's not only retained most of the faithful black audience cultivated by the Revue, she's increased it by attracting the beat-box and hip-hop generation, who neither saw nor heard the early stuff. New wavers and punks, fashion trendies, Yuppies and Bumps (black upwardly mobile professionals), young and old, all worship at her shrine.

Tina Turner's emergence in the eighties as a major musical force represents an extremely shrewd merger of carefully manipulated image projection and substantial, creative output. Tina has consented to being typecast as a screaming long-legged beauty while singing songs that question the value of that very image and criticize those who'd make character assumptions based on the image. At forty-six she's a heroic figure: an abused wife with guts enough to walk away from a seemingly idyllic union and remake her career, a singer willing to risk or accept ridicule from her own people by insisting on doing allegedly white music after developing a following within traditional black pop structures. Rock in the eighties is a predominantly white, macho-posturing, teen-oriented music, no matter how much journalists claim its appeal is more diversified, so her popularity stands as an even more amazing reality. Her appeal can't be chalked up just to looks alone or to the fact that she's a lone black woman rock singer. Both Vanity and Sheila E. are more visually stunning and Wendy O. Williams certainly portrays a more other-worldly figure than Tina. But Tina's a phenomenon, an artist whose success defies quick explanations and whose earning potential and across-the-board popularity are limitless at this moment in history.

Private Dancer, the album that launched the ascendence of Tina Turner, was in the Top 10 of the black and pop charts for

CURT GUNTHER/CAMERA 5

months. The album's signature piece, "What's Love Got to Do with It," was a triple-platinum single, topping the black, pop, and dance charts during the summer of 1984. Other singles from the LP, "Let's Stay Together," "You'd Better Be Good to Me," and the title cut have crossed over to black, white, and Latin buyers and registered well with audiences across the sexual and age spectrums.

A 1966 publicity shot issued by I.& T.T. Productions, Inc.

Tina prepares to propel the crowd into a frenzy before a 1975 outdoor concert in Los Angeles.

More importantly than mere sales figures, Tina Turner breaks rules and flaunts the conventions that have both subtly and overtly forced black women to conduct themselves in a less assertive, distinctive manner than their white counterparts. Tina is sultry, sensual, aggressive; she openly tailors her performance to take advantage of male fantasies and makes no apologies for it. She has customized her own form of expression but is honest enough to shrug aside any notion that her own identity may be jeopardized by the stage image. She also knows and exploits the power of media and the attraction of music videos. She moves from soft-spoken, barely audible interviews on radio shows like "Special Edition" to in-depth, grueling interviews on "20/20" and then

SIMON FOWLER/RETNA

In the mid-seventies

onto show-stopping, riveting performances in usually pro forma lip synch appearances on TV's "Solid Gold" or "American Bandstand." Above all else, Tina Turner is hip, stays current, and has the sense of style and flair that all great performers project effortlessly.

Tina Turner was one of a number of performers who turned my house into a battlefield during my adolescent years. Neither of my parents viewed music outside the church as anything other than a useless field dominated by illiterates and homosexuals, one that whites were quite happy to let blacks waste time with at the expense of developing their mental capacities. My growing passion for music, satisfied through constant visits to record stores with meager resources and long nights curled up with a cheap radio, was greeted with disdain, threats, and occasional physical response—if a musical interlude interrupted a homework session.

WLAC-AM radio in Nashville, Tennessee, first brought Tina Turner into my life. The station was a 50,000-watt clear-channel butt-kicker; in the daytime its fare was mainly country, but at night the menu was classic southern soul and gutbucket R&B. Amidst the pitches for skin lightener, hair oils, and the latest 45s from Ernie's and Randy's Record Shops came "A Fool in Love." Hoss Allen screamed, "IT'S A HIT!" and the dual impact of his enthusiasm and Tina's vocal majesty caused me to knock my cheap radio on the floor, shattering it resoundingly.

In the ensuing years I've followed Tina through the ups and downs—endured the wretched solo albums in the seventies, suffered through the unreal, Twilight Zone "acting" in *Tommy*, and finally rejoiced at her triumph, even though some aspects of the contemporary Tina Turner disturb me.

Those of us who matured in the soul era have had to make peace with Tina's embrace of rock. For many of us, the term *rock & roll* holds little meaning other than as a generic term

DAVID REDFERN/RETNA

whites use to classify and remove certain music out of the realm of black creation and into some nether world of pseudo-integration. Tina knows full well that black audiences supported her long before she and Ike left for England, and yet some of her early interviews after "Let's Stay Together" became a hit read like veiled put-downs of that audience. To be fair, she's since cleared up any misconceptions that she hates R&B or has rejected her roots. When you hear her speak, you know she came from Nutbush, Tennessee, not Southampton. Her face has finally begun appearing on supermarket tabloids, and public demand has forced her to frequent the hangouts where inventive "journalists" hover to get their phony information. She doesn't live the gaudy lifestyle that gets slobbered over on tripe like "Lifestyles of the Rich and Famous." Tina's glamorous but not phony, good-natured but no pushover.

No one would tag Tina with the misused innovator label. It's fairly easy to trace the blues and soul influences on her style and to hear the black church's influence in her delivery and articulation. Her dancing and stage movements are incredible, but they're not revolutionary in the way that James Brown and Jackie Wilson brought athletic agility to the concert setting.

Through the sixties I saw the Revue as often as possible, and I followed them religiously in the seventies. But the records became less and less interesting with time, and rumors circulated about trouble in paradise. However, that didn't affect the live show until the early seventies. When Tina finally left the group, my reaction was classic out-to-lunch analysis—I told friends that her career was over and time would vindicate Ike as the real genius. Tina Turner was a great performer but would never make it on her own without Ike's sure-handed direction, I foolishly asserted.

My reaction could be chalked up to sexism or ignorance; I underrated her abilities. Growing up with your standard male biases and the reinforcement of seventeen years of Southern Baptist dogma to hone them, I'm certain I had a host of stereotyped notions about women as conceptual artists. At times these resurface; years of fighting to rid myself of them only help me to see just how deeply they were ingrained (you've got to admit to a bias to remedy it). At any rate, when "Let's Stay Together" first hit the airwaves, I knew my summation of Tina's career chances were way out of whack. She took a soul standard and inverted it as emphatically as Aretha Franklin took Otis Redding's "Respect" and made folks think she'd patented that. Tina stretched out the notes, phrased the lyrics, and gave them a dramatic ardor that sliced up Al Green's masterpiece in ways previously deemed impossible. The splitting clarity of her voice and the range of emotion she displayed allowed her to execute each line without an ounce of pretentiousness. Sophistication rubbed shoulders with earthiness, and Tina Turner leaped over the pack to assume the throne.

When the "Let's Stay Together" video finally appeared and Tina flashed onto the screen with moves that fused sensuality, sprightliness, and house-rocking revivalism, my last doubts vanished. She had refined some of the things from her Revue years into a setting as with-it as quiche but as down-home as grits. When the subsequent single "What's Love Got to Do with It" was released, the puzzle's final piece fell into place. Now she'd reworked the image as well. No longer was Tina Turner only a whirling, sexy shouter; now she could be a sensitive, compelling spokeswoman as well, voicing provocative and disturbing sentiments in a song without sacrificing the lure and electricity of her prior material. Tina Turner had made the step from contributor to presenter to controller; she was totally in charge—esthetically and musically.

There have been a lot of years and myriad social changes since my first encounter with Tina Turner. Sadly, much of the poverty and social injustice that permeated the environments where I admired her as a teenager remains unchanged. But Tina has moved beyond the frontiers of late-night black radio and onto the playlists of the Z-100's and VJ's. She's heard on CHR, AOR, Top 40, Urban, even the handful of stations that dare call themselves black these days. In short, Tina's the queen of all she surveys and then some. This is her story up to now, viewed through the eyes of someone happy about her success while still fondly remembering the gloriousness of her past.

CHAPTER ONE

"Private Dancer"

Tina Turner was born Anna Mae Bullock, on November 26, 1939, in Nutbush, Tennessee, a small town located between Jackson and Memphis. The town's size can be viewed in two relative ways: Many longtime Tennesseans have either never heard of it or are not sure where it's located, and many state maps don't show it anywhere.

The Bullocks were a sharecropping family, like so many black and white families in the Delta, and Tina's early days were spent alongside her father, Floyd, a Baptist minister, picking cotton and strawberries. The sharecropper existence, eking out a bare living from the soil, is not one Tina recalls very bitterly, to judge by her comments on it: "We always had nice furniture and our house was always nice. We [she and her sister, Eileen] had our own separate bedroom and a dining room, and we had pigs and animals. I knew the people who didn't, so I knew what being poor was like. And we weren't poor."

Anna Mae attended a two-room grammar school in Nutbush. The bulk of her spare and weekend time was spent in

A Liberty Records publicity shot

her father's Baptist church. She sang in the choir but says she wasn't particularly gifted or outstanding at that time. Beyond that, Tina's recollections of her childhood are filled with digs and cracks about her appearance. She says she didn't really do that much dating, wasn't very pleased with how she looked, and was very introverted. She also remembers taking numerous fad remedies to build up her body and bust—without success.

Music became her outlet for personal expression. She not only sang gospel on Sundays but learned blues and country tunes from radio broadcasts from stations like WDIA in Memphis, with Nat D. Williams, and WLAC from Nashville, with Big John R. Ernie and Hoss Allen. A few years later these same stations would be instruments through which Tina and Ike established themselves as viable and popular performers.

Tina remains conspicuously silent about her family relations. Apparently she and her sister, Eileen, were close. But her parents split in 1956 when she was a teen-ager, her mother going to St. Louis and her father to Chicago. She comments on this only to say, "There were some problems," but the details are missing. Anna and Eileen went to St. Louis with their mother, and Nutbush became just a memory, although the poignant strains and lyrics of her later song "Nutbush City Limits," on which she shared the writing credit with Ike, are an indication that Anna Mae Bullock never forgot the town completely.

St. Louis was a whole new world from Nutbush, Tennessee. It was a major metropolitan city with a sprawling, wide-open night life. It was also a major source of blues and R&B artists, with several clubs regularly featuring such acts as Albert King, Little Milton, Johnny O'Neal, Oliver Sain, and Ike Turner. East St. Louis, right across the Mississippi River, was even more of a boomtown for music. Its clubs and taverns didn't all close promptly at 1 A.M.

CURT GUNTHER/CAMERA 5

Tina in the early days, a time during which she saw herself as all torso and legs

There were live broadcasts on KATZ radio from several area clubs: the Moonlight Lounge, the Dynaflow, the Club Imperial, the Club Riviera, and the West End Waiters in St. Louis; the Club Manhatten (sic), the Blue Note, and the Sportsman in East St. Louis; Kingbury's in Madison, Illinois; and Perry's Lounge in Eagle Park. There were even a few small record labels. The biggest was Bobbin, but there was also Planet, Norman, Royal American Ultrasonic, Joyce, and Tune Town, producing down-home records (for blacks with roots in the rural South), blues singles, a few novelty numbers, and even some vocal groups. No St. Louis label ever achieved the staying power of Chess in Chicago or Sun in Memphis, but they did serve a useful purpose in getting area talent recorded, launching careers and contributing to the overall development of the St. Louis–East St. Louis entertainment scene.

MICK ROCK

Ike Turner—bandleader, guitarist, composer, and one-time talent scout. In 1985 he was reported to have approached Teena Marie with a proposition that would have led to the Ike and Teena Revue.

Eileen and Anna Mae Bullock went to all the clubs as often as possible. Eileen was at first the more avid goer, but after some initial coaxing, Anna became as steady and enthusiastic a club follower as her sister. One of the acts that Anna immediately became impressed with was headed by a bandleader/musician named Ike Turner, who'd been in St. Louis since 1954.

Ike had recorded for Vita, Federal, Tune Town, and Cobra but was currently without a record contract. He was a versatile if unpredictable composer and player; reportedly he once made a country record under the name Icky Reinrut to evade the exclusivity stricture that Sun Records had put on his services. His Kings of Rhythm band, which he'd been leading in one fashion or another since 1951, was one of the busiest bands in the area, and its personnel included at one time or another vocalists Jimmy Turner and Bobby Foster, guitarists Johnny Wright and Timothy Cooper (the latter also on harmonica), and saxophonists Raymond Hill and Glenn White. Songs by the group, such as "Jack Rabbit" and "Angel of Love," were heavily played in the St. Louis area, and Ike enjoyed the kind of local hero-worship accorded many regional black stars in the segregation era.

The Club Manhatten wasn't a particularly large place; but the fact it frequently stayed open all night and was usually filled with a mixture of partygoers, curiosity seekers, unsavory types, and many people from across the river made it a prime East St. Louis hotspot. Eileen Bullock had gone there several times and come away impressed. Her vivid descriptions and coaxing led Anna to join her and they became regulars at the club; Anna had just turned seventeen and was ready to enjoy the things Nutbush couldn't offer. It was at the Club Manhatten that she first saw Ike Turner.

DAVID REDFERN/RETNA

Ike was usually content to remain in the background during performances by the Revue and, for that matter, the Kings of Rhythm. This shot, taken during a Revue performance, captures him laying down one of the rippling backgrounds that fortified Tina's vocals.

SIMON FOWLER/RETNA

Anna's first reaction upon seeing Ike was one of fascination. She was drawn to his smooth presence on stage and attracted by the kind of music his band made: propulsive but not overwhelming, powerful yet soothing. After the second set Eileen and Anna went backstage, and Anna gingerly broached to Ike the possibility of coming on stage and singing with the band one night. Ike was quite amenable to the suggestion. Sure, he told her, only he didn't say what night.

After a few nights of sitting and waiting for the call that didn't come, Anna took matters into her own hands. One evening she simply jumped onstage, grabbed the microphone, and started singing. While she had entered talent shows back in Nutbush, what Anna knew about singing was minimal. She knew how to project her voice and wail from the Baptist Church, but she didn't know about microphone technique, stage movement, or dynamics. Nevertheless, her aggressiveness (out of character for her at that time) and raw talent impressed Ike. He didn't hire her on the spot but began letting her do some singing with the group at the Club Manhatten and at other places on other evenings.

Ike began working up ideas on how to use this seventeen-year-old's developing talent. Although he hadn't yet hit on the idea that would ultimately yield the Revue, he started to slide Anna up front, began featuring her and doing occasional duets with her. More importantly, he began building the seeds of a personal and professional relationship.

Tina talks about how she became influenced by Ike at this early point—how he became a father, mentor, and overseer wrapped in one. "I became like a star. I felt real special. Ike went out and bought me stage clothes—a fur, gloves up to here, costume jewelry and baseball pumps, glittery shoes, large earrings and form-fitting dresses. And I was wearing a padded bra. I thought I was so sharp. And riding in this

NANCY BARR/RETNA

Cadillac Ike had then—a pink Fleetwood with the fish fins. I swear, I felt like I was rich. And it felt real good."

Suddenly the small-town girl from Nutbush was in the big time, going across first the St. Louis area and then across the Southeast and Delta. They weren't yet ready to make records, even though Ike continued cutting demos at his home studio. Anna kept doing her few numbers each night.

Then in 1957 that changed. Ike hired her as an official member of the Kings of Rhythm. The first phase was complete. Anna Mae Bullock had become a professional, a regular member of a touring band. A host of things both pleasant and unpleasant awaited. The next step was the transformation of the Kings of Rhythm and Anna Mae Bullock into the Ike and Tina Turner Revue. That came in 1960. When they cut the demo for "A Fool in Love," Ike turned it in as done by "Ike and Tina Turner." (The name *Tina* supposedly came via a modification of *Sheena,* the name of the lead character in a 1950s B-movie, *Sheena of the Jungle*.) Anna apparently wasn't consulted on the change, but whether she was or not, she evidently accepted it immediately. Tina Turner was on her way.

Tina enjoys one of the luxuries of fame as well as some time away from the spotlight.

CURT GUNTHER/CAMERA 5

CHAPTER TWO

"Fool in Love"

The Sensational Ike and Tina Turner Revue featuring Tina Turner and the Ikettes, later shortened by virtually all fans and chroniclers to the Ike and Tina Turner Revue, was an outgrowth of Ike's superb Kings of Rhythm band. This was actually the second edition of the Kings of Rhythm; the initial group had formed in 1950 and recorded in Memphis with blues and later rockabilly impresario Sam Phillips in 1951. One of the songs, a blaring number with a sputtering, wailing lead vocal by Jackie Brenston was called "Rocket 88." This song not only became a Number One hit in 1951 but later caused a split in the ranks, with Brenston and the group leaving Ike and heading to Chicago.

Ike, a Clarksville, Mississippi, native, regrouped. First he hooked up with Lester Bihari of RPM/Modern records, who employed him as a talent scout, a role Ike utilized to tour the South and record numerous artists, including Elmore James. More importantly, he eventually wound up in East St. Louis in 1955, left Modern, and reestablished the Kings of Rhythm, cutting some items for the Federal label and gaining exposure and popularity in the area. Ike built his own studio in his home and spent countless hours making demo records and experimenting with vocalists in his group. This background would prove critical. Years before Ike ever met Tina Turner nee Anna Mae Bullock, he had a polished, firm sense of what he wanted his orchestras and bands to sound like and how he wanted his vocalists to interact within that concept. While it's certainly true that Tina's dogged persistence, remarkable talents, and physical prowess were partially, if not totally responsible for Ike's decision to rework the Kings of Rhythm around her, it's also true that he had a strong, unyielding idea of how he felt she should be presented, of what kinds of things the Revue could do best with her as its principal vocalist, and what her role should be. Ike didn't

MICHAEL OCHS ARCHIVES

Tina pauses to let Ike take the spotlight for one brief moment, this time on guitar.

create a Revue for Tina; he carved out a niche for her and determined at all times what it would be. The duo's marriage in 1962 only served to cement Ike's position as the determiner of Tina's destiny offstage and on. He chose the music, decided what routines were included and which got excised, picked the rotating members of the Ikettes, and in general ran the show.

Tina now virtually refuses to comment on her Revue days. But it's clear from the information assembled through various accounts and her past utterances that she had virtually no input into the daily workings of the Revue.

They were the ultimate chitlin' circuit touring ensemble; they appeared in dirt-floor clubs in such southern paradises as Griffin, Georgia, and Tupelo, Mississippi. While most white fans' remembrances of Ike and Tina Turner begin with 1969 and their performances on the Rolling Stones tour, southern black audiences packed auditoriums to see them throughout the sixties. My own recollections of the Revue include a pair of mid-sixties concerts I attended in my hometown of Knoxville, Tennessee. Both times the energy generated emotions that ranged from frightening to astonishing. When the curtain rose, the announcer/MC screamed, "THE IKE AND TINA TURNER REVUE!" whereupon Tina and the Ikettes entered doing a shimmy routine and then undulated through a torrid opening number; instant emotional Armaggedon ensued.

One of the allegations I find most puzzling about the Revue is that Tina somehow never got a chance really to sing or reveal her talents. Some of this has come from Tina herself, particularly in interviews in which she's talked about her joy at getting a chance to sing Beatles and Stones material in the early seventies. "For the first time I really got a chance to sing, to do something besides screech and holler," she told "Entertainment Tonight" during an interview in 1984 and again during a segment shot after the Grammy Awards broadcast in early 1985. Yet I can remember her singing everything from "Please, Please, Please" to slow blues and even a backwater country ballad in Revue concerts.

Furthermore, it was crystal clear to anyone who ever saw the Revue live that Tina was the star. Ike, whatever his behavior offstage, took a markedly secondary role onstage. He frequently let other band members take solos and re-

MICHAEL OCHS ARCHIVES

mained slightly to the side most of the show, adding the occasional guitar lick, bass riff, or piano fill. When Ike did step forward, he moved with careful precision, extra-long guitar chord dangling in the rear. His exchanges with Tina were complementary in nature. Sure, there would be times when the excitement of the moment might cause the voices to up the intensity, but he was for all intents and purposes a foil for Tina to work off of, just as the Ikettes were.

The Revue always skittered along on the fine line between spontaneity and precision. A great deal of the antics were executed so crisply that a sophisticated observer would know there'd been extensive preparation beforehand; yet during the Revue's heyday Ike and Tina could convey enough of an air of looseness and stir up so much reaction that no one even thought about its being rehearsed.

Indeed, it was the degeneration of the live performances that provided the first clues to the discord that was disintegrating the marriage. By the mid-seventies the Ike and Tina Turner Revues were no longer events, they were disasters. Bits that once were performed with a sense of flair and dramatic verve now looked turgid and weary. My final view of the group in its last days came at a 1971 concert in Massachusetts. It was a brutal, dispirited event despite Tina's game efforts to keep everything together. The dance steps didn't have their customary vigor, Ike stayed to the side for the bulk of the evening, and a skeletal Revue minus horn section played with all the conviction of a studio band five minutes from the end of a marathon session.

When the allegations of mistreatment and abuse finally surfaced, it wasn't hard to understand why the Revue fell apart. There had always been a disturbing quality of subservience permeating the Revue. I suppose I could not articulate it at the time, since these notions were beyond the realm of a fourteen-year-old in the mid-sixties still torn by his parents' assertions that the Revue's music was low-life patter best reserved for the kind of folks who spent Saturday nights cutting each other up and getting carted off in ambulances and paddy wagons. However, I also think that most of us in the Revue's audiences in the sixties thought only about the music's impact. We reacted, danced, shouted, and swayed with no thought given to what the performers on stage were feeling. This wasn't something new or endemic to my generation, but it's something that Tina Turner's emergence as a

JOCHEN BAEUERLE

MICHAEL OCHS ARCHIVES

Although the end was near for both the Revue and the marriage, you couldn't detect it in the enthusiasm displayed here during a 1976 performance.

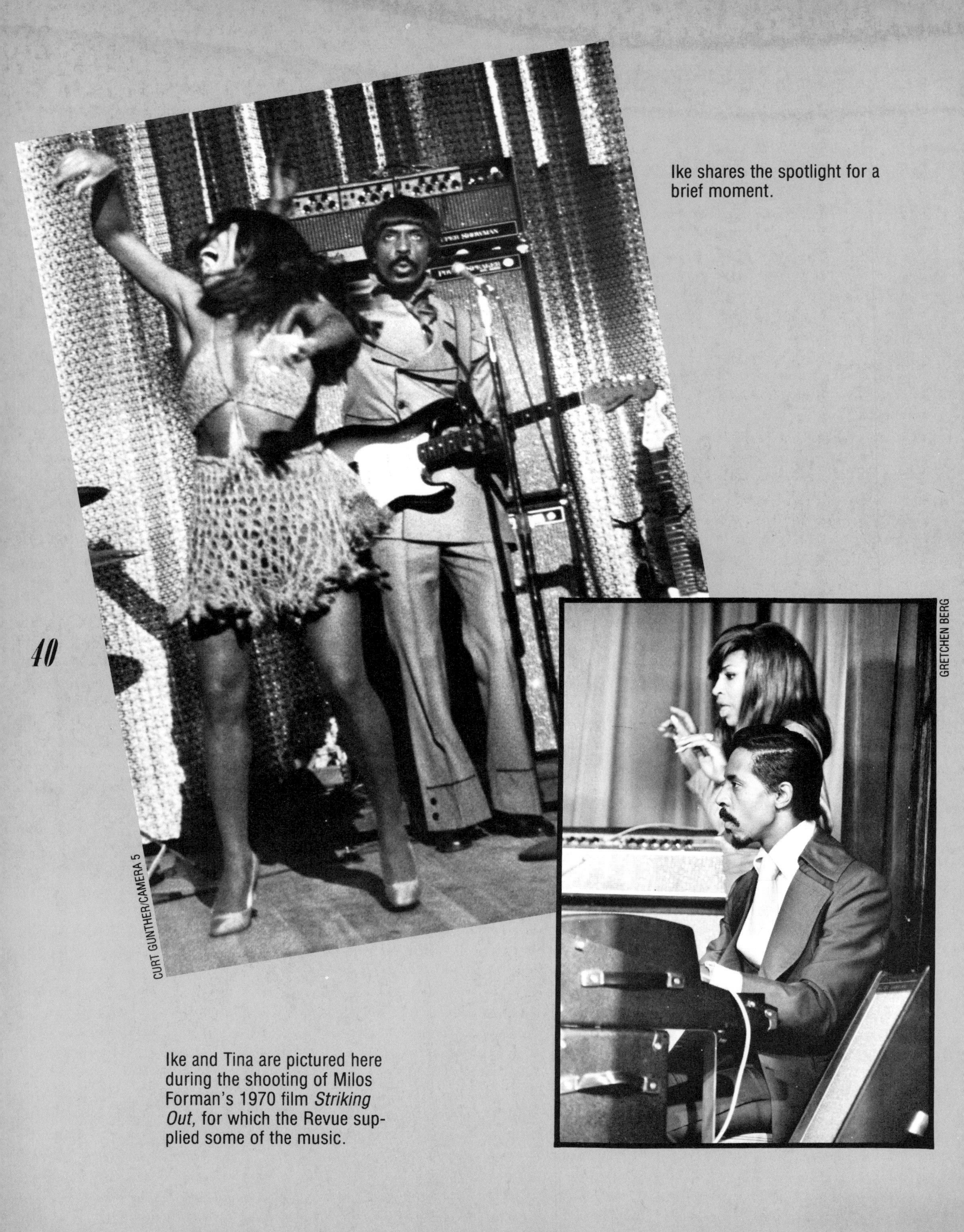
CURT GUNTHER/CAMERA 5

GRETCHEN BERG

Ike shares the spotlight for a brief moment.

Ike and Tina are pictured here during the shooting of Milos Forman's 1970 film *Striking Out,* for which the Revue supplied some of the music.

PAUL CANTY/RETNA

superstar has helped correct somewhat, and it's something that she had to break out of the Revue environment to combat. Ultimately, no matter how great she was as a member of Ike and Tina Turner's Revue, outside the Revue she was still not acknowledged, considered, or evaluated by the audience as someone with something important to say. She could only be the consummate cog in the wheel; today she's the entire car.

While the Revue's musical menu emphasized spicy, saucy, up-tempo numbers, Tina did get a chance over a period of

MICHAEL OCHS ARCHIVES

An early newspaper photo shows Anna Mae Bullock rehearsing with Ike Turner.

Ike's Liberty Records publicity photo, taken in the early seventies.

time to sing enough material to stretch out her voice. The prominent delivery; mastery of the lower and middle ranges, heard most clearly on *Private Dancer;* and her keen ability to articulate clearly and cleanly at high peaks were certainly honed through nights of screaming and wailing. Ike may have put too much of a premium on making Tina holler; in fact, much of the early seventies presentations that thrilled white audiences had Tina screeching so loudly that you wondered if she knew what she was singing. But overall, Tina's vocal abilities were well served by her stint with the Revue.

On the other hand, nuance, subtlety, versatility were not characteristics of the dance routines Tina and the Ikettes performed nightly. There's no question that Tina and the Ikettes could whip across a stage and do a routine capable of

MICHAEL OCHS ARCHIVES

burning down a stage, but that was all you ever saw them do. The Tina/Ikettes segment finally got as worn out as some of the steps that standup vocal groups had perfected during Motown's heyday. It's highly ironic that one of the most graceful, agile dancers of all time would be confined in an area where some imagination could have resulted in dance history.

Fortunately the Ike and Tina Turner Revue is one of the acts preserved on the superb video program *That Was Rock: The T.A.M.I./T.N.T. Show*. Even though they are only shown doing three numbers, every element of the Revue at its peak is on display. Tina whirls, moans, swoops, steps, and moves into the audience to get some reaction and exchange quips, finally breaking into a torrid high-step and dress-swirling routine with the Ikettes during an instrumental interlude. She sings "Please, Please, Please" one more time and switches the supplication and emphasis until the audience is begging her and she's answering them back. There's also an exchange in which Ike makes his way to the microphone, extra-long cord hanging prominently in the back, adds his own "ooh-wah, ooh-wahs," and then slips back into the band. It's a short but hypnotic glimpse of the Revue at a time when it rivaled James Brown's Revue for bragging rights of the deep South.

The Ike and Tina Turner Revue finally degenerated. Tina simply possessed too much vocal and physical talent to stay locked into a thematic concept that she had no control over or little interest in maintaining. Yet the Revue's greatness as a performing ensemble should not be minimized; it fused fifties rock-boogie with gospel fervor and jump band organization and was the training ground from which Tina Turner would later emerge renewed and reborn.

LFI/RETNA

CHAPTER THREE

"It's Gonna Work Out Fine"

The Ike and Tina Turner Revue was neither a major hitmaker nor a resounding failure. It scored a sizable number of hits in the early sixties, went through a dry spell, and then bounced back during the late sixties to score more chart successes, although their records became more inconsistent and uneven as the seventies progressed.

The definitive Ike and Tina records were the early ones they made for the Sue label. Their first hit, "A Fool in Love," marked Tina's vinyl debut as the principal vocalist of the Revue, and featured what would be the theme of most of the Sue material: the triumph of love over domestic difficulties. They enjoyed four other smash hits on Sue between 1960 and 1963: "It's Gonna Work Out Fine" in 1961 and "I Idolize You" that same year, and then two more big sellers in 1962, "Poor Fool" and "Tra La La La La." Tina was not yet a polished, confident singer, but her ability to take sentimental love song fare and stretch out lines, interjecting dimensions of passion and qualities of expressiveness seemingly beyond the lyric capacity of the material, was already impressive.

Tina clowns around during an early 1970s concert date.

What's also striking about the Sue work is the sound of her voice. There's a tenderness, a sense of innocence that altered radically through the years and disappeared completely by the time the Revue splintered.

If any song lyrically outlined the way Tina felt about Ike during that period it was "I Idolize You." Tina could very well have been revealing her own feelings about Ike as she outlined the story of a lover who admired her mate immensely, overlooked his transgressions, and stood faithful to the end. While the musical background for the Sue sides was usually stomping, driving fare, the arrangement for "Think It's Gonna Work Out Fine" blended an almost melodramatic, sweeping refrain and chorus with a terse, husky delivery by Tina and unflappable harmonizing by Ike.

After leaving Sue, Ike reacquainted himself with Lester Bihari, and the Revue spent two years recording for Modern, excluding a short period with Loma, which yielded two superb live albums and the exciting single "Tell Her I'm Not Home." All these Loma productions were supervised by the legendary "Bumps" Blackwell, the man who presided over the greatest recordings Little Richard ever made. Neither Loma album made much pop chart noise, but they were state-of-the-art Revue LPs. Tina's in-concert raps and quips to the audience were included, and the Revue's kinetic, bristling musical support backed her superbly.

The 1963–65 Modern period was one of steady recording and sporadic chart entry. "Goodbye So Long" was perhaps their best Modern single, but there were several others of note: "If I Can't Be First," "Something Came Over Me," and "I Can't Believe What You Say." There were also some incredibly prophetic numbers recorded in this stint, songs that lyrically seemed to portend the happenings of 1975. "Hurt Is All You Gave Me" spells out a troubled relationship marked by the man's inability to do anything except hurt the

The Revue, with the happy couple at rear, poses for the Spud "Nik" Booking Agency publicity photo.

woman. "Don't You Blame It on Me" details an independent spirit and unwillingness to accept unfounded charges that certainly were part of Tina's resolve to end her marriage and start over. Even the uncertainty echoed in "Am I a Fool in Love?" may have generated in her own mind some questions about her situation. While the defection would not occur for another decade, lyrically one can hear and discern some of the seeds of disenchantment being sown. This doesn't mean Tina Turner was being turned into a disgruntled, disillusioned individual merely by singing particular numbers, but it does indicate that certain songs the Revue made in the

LFI/RETNA

The Ikettes occupy center stage for a moment in this shot, sans Ike, Tina, or Revue.

LIAISON

This time Tina joins the Ikettes for their patterned routine.

CURT GUNTHER/CAMERA 5

Tina and the Ikettes let it fly.

MICK ROCK

period 1963–65 may have sparked some thoughts by Tina regarding her own situation.

The Revue spent a short period of time on Ray Charles's Tangerine label before being approached by Phil Spector. He'd worked with the Revue on the T.N.T. show and had been greatly impressed. Spector gave them a $20,000 advance to get a release from Tangerine and then spent another $25,000 recording and mixing the sessions that yielded the controversial *River Deep, Mountain High* LP for Phillies Records in 1966. The album was the final "wall-of-sound" production for Spector and has been much discussed in terms of its lack of U.S. acceptance. The song was a Top 10 smash in England and led to a tour of that nation in 1966 that began with a hero's welcome. *River Deep* marked the start of a love affair between the British and Tina Turner that still continues today, despite the fact that soul traditionalists at British publications like *Black Echoes* disdain the direction of her contemporary material. The Revue appeared on television and gave concerts all over England before sold-out, highly appreciative audiences.

But while *River Deep* may have been a crucial record in terms of introducing the Revue to a new audience outside the realm of the chitlin' circuit, it was not a complete artistic success. Spector's wall-of-sound production does not completely mesh with Tina's bluesy, sultry vocals. The title track works marvelously, but the other items on the album seem disjointed and in conflict. Tina sounds rushed and confined by the production. *River Deep* should have been a major success as a single; as a complete album it's a disappointment. Spector apparently didn't understand how the Revue functioned or what kind of backgrounds suited Tina's voice.

The UA recordings from the early seventies represent the best work the Revue produced in its final years. Released on a variety of labels, these songs, particularly "Proud Mary" in 1971 as well as covers of "Come Together," "Honky-Tonk

CURT GUNTHER/CAMERA 5

Woman," "Get Back," and others signaled the beginning of the end for the Revue and the start of a new phase for Tina. She found an excitement, an openness in the material of rock writers that she felt had been missing in the Revue's repertoire. Furthermore, she could give these songs new interpretations, shadings, and inflections, because her background was so different from that of the songs' composers. Her rendition of "Proud Mary" had a churning vitality completely removed from the country-inflected reading John Fogerty had given it in his original version. And the Beatles' mystical performance of "Come Together" is hardly echoed by Tina's shout-and-testify, confrontational performance.

These songs also demonstrated the fact that Tina didn't need Ike or the Revue. While he was an integral part of "Proud Mary," with a bluesy chorus sung underneath Tina's assertion that "We never do anything easy!", on "Come Together" and "Honky-Tonk Woman" he only seemed to get in

The Ikettes pose for a United Artists publicity still after they joined the label in 1971.

LFI/RETNA

One of the key events of the Revue's history was its appearance on the British television showcase "Ready, Steady, Go!" which boosted their already high popularity in England and marked Tina's first concert in front of British audiences.

the way. These songs now demanded the assertiveness of one person, not a lead singer reined in by the parameters of a group. However, it can be claimed that these songs lacked the pulsating musical character of the Ike and Tina Turner work from the Sue, Modern, and Loma era. There were no remarkable fuzz-tone solos to the rock pieces, no jutting horn lines or saucy backbeat. For fans of the old Revue it marked a sad moment in music history, but for Tina admirers it was a time to celebrate. At last she was beginning to exhibit qualities of a complete vocalist: versatility in doing songs some felt were indelibly for (white) rock artists and adaptability in taking lyrics and situations written for others and personalizing them.

Most of what the Ike and Tina Turner Revue recorded after 1971 was forgettable. Compilations and greatest hits albums turned up repeatedly; the best original album they made before the split was 1973's *Nutbush City Limits*, with a powerful performance by Tina on the autobiographical title track qualifying as a suitable good-bye to the Revue. She left the Revue and Ike two years later; and they were divorced in 1976.

In evaluating the music of the Revue, it's clear that Ike's domination took its toll on Tina's performance. The sense of drudgery, the raspy edge in her voice, and the contrasting feeling of euphoria clearly evident in the rock covers indicates that Tina knew years before she left the Revue that she was locked into a musical dead end. The Revue made its best records when Tina was still relatively new to the group. Constant touring, repetition of routines, and recording songs selected solely by Ike finally drained the group's recording power, though the live shows didn't start showing the strains until much later. However, one can easily question Tina's assertion that her embrace of rock music was a key factor in her decision to bolt the Revue. Rock music did play a part in showing her that she could function outside the group, and it had tremendous appeal for her as a solo artist. But the domination by Ike, the grind of the Revue, and weariness with the abuse she reportedly endured were far more pivotal and crucial elements in her decision, even though she now professes almost complete disdain for the music of her past.

The Ike and Tina Revue truly functioned best as a performing ensemble. No album or single, even the finest hits and live LPs, really communicated anything remotely close to the feelings they could generate live. The Revue made far better singles than albums; the single could condense the ensemble's inspirational bursts, while the album dispersed them and also illuminated the defects and cliches. Increasingly the Revue's records showed Tina battling to go beyond the limits that Ike wanted maintained; the tension made the records even steamier than usual.

A flood of both reissues and newly released material since 1984 has resulted in a great deal of the Revue's work being made available for the first time in quite a while. However, the Sue selections continue to rank as the finest of the Revue's released work. Unfortunately, they are domestically unavailable except on expensive import albums from Germany.

Whether the Ike and Tina Turner Revue albums and singles remain in print or not, and whether their memory will someday be obliterated by the impact of Tina's post-Revue material remains to be seen. Anyone with even a remote interest in Tina Turner's career should seek out these recordings. For all their unevenness and musical similarity, they do document the beginning, development, and fruition of a singer who would later become a superstar by daring to break with the stylistic conventions that had enabled her to develop her talent in the first place.

BOB LEAFE

NEAL PRESTON/CAMERA 5

CHAPTER FOUR

"You Shoulda Treated Me Right"

There was nothing very simple about the relationship between Ike and Tina Turner. It began in an unequal fashion and grew steadily worse as the years progressed, until Tina made the decision to break away and establish her independence. Although they were married for nearly twelve years, Tina never speaks of fond—or romantic—remembrances of Ike. She will admit to his business acumen and talk about his musical knowledge, but lacking from her interviews is any mention of warm, tender feelings—just briefly recounted tales of exploitation and abuse.

The two became romantically involved in 1960, growing closer in the wake of the success of their first hit, "A Fool in Love." Tina hadn't really wanted to grow close to Ike in this way; she had more or less looked upon him as another father figure or adviser. She's admitted that initially she was hesitant when Ike started approaching and relating to her in a sexual manner. She also had fears about what involvement would do to their status as performers. Ike had a questionable reputation in terms of dealings with women, and she didn't

Tina poses for a 1982 studio shot.

especially relish the possibility of joining the list. Ike and his common-law wife had split up, reconciled, and split again during Tina's early days in the Revue, and seeing this soap opera acted out in front of her didn't exactly reassure her about Ike. "I remember some nights when he would have maybe six girl friends in the house [i.e., waiting for him in the audience] and he would stay up there and call his wife to come to the club that night. It was the only way they could save him"—from the inevitable scene his jealous girl friends would create.

Nevertheless, misgivings and all, Ike and Tina were married in 1962 in Mexico at 4:55 P.M. on a Friday. The ceremony was held in a fleabag hotel and lacked even the glamor of a marriage at City Hall. Tina remembers insects crawling around and the whole affair resembling a bad "Twilight Zone" episode.

Worse, Tina was already having doubts about her place in the Revue, Ike's influence on her life, and the submergence of her personality. "When he asked me to marry him, I didn't want to, because I knew then what my life would be like. But I was afraid to say no. I was still in love, but I was beginning to realize I was unhappy. I didn't want the relationship anymore. It started that early. We were two totally different people." Thus what was already a troubled professional union became an even more troubled marriage, with Ike now completely in the driver's seat, emotionally and professionally.

Ike had a reputation in St. Louis music circles for being tough. It came with the territory; characters like Houston music impresario and restaurant owner Don Robey (owner of Duke Records) were known for their ruthlessness, and the venues on the chitlin' circuit didn't exactly resemble country clubs. Ike was also a perfectionist and demanding taskmaster with a very short fuse and fierce disposition.

LIAISON

All these things came to the fore quickly in the marriage. A period of extreme difficulty began, one that would finally run its course with Tina reportedly just refusing to be slapped around anymore and willingly taking steps that would plunge her into a period of tenuous finances and artistic chaos. At any rate, Tina's revelations of Ike's abuse shocked almost every observer. There had been rumors floating around for years that Ike treated her unfairly, but most of these centered around his countless one-night affairs.

Tina has admitted to one suicide attempt, and in at least one interview offered some terrifying evidence about Ike's reaction. ". . . I was in the hospital [after taking the pills] and I heard later from the doctor they couldn't get a pulse. And apparently Ike came in and started talking to me. Ike said, 'You motherfucker, you better not die; I'll kill you'—and my pulse started."

The most baffling thing about the Ike and Tina situation remains Tina's endurance of it for so long. Fear, admiration, even love don't really provide adequate explanations, and Tina herself hasn't totally addressed the question, even though she does chalk a lot up to the fact that they were making money and she wasn't assertive and confident enough to think she could make it on her own.

It's highly ironic that Tina's suffering has played a role in her being so heavily admired. Had she simply abandoned Ike three months after the abuse began, it seems unlikely that she would be idolized as the woman who endured and finally triumphed. Her insistence on being a strong character, performing in a very physical way, and keeping up with the times can also be traced back to the Revue days and the years spent with Ike. She knows she allowed herself to be bullied, subordinated, and led around and has vowed it will never happen again. She can be both a representation of the liberated, in-charge, with-it woman of the eighties and a

MICHAEL OCHS ARCHIVES

MICK ROCK

Tina and the Ikettes strut their stuff.

symbol of the historic inhumanity men have dished out to women.

Yet Tina's smart enough to know that even the most sympathetic fan won't respond to bitterness and/or innuendo. She has not used the platforms of big-time media to wrap Ike, nor has she ever done anything other than lay out the basic scenario. In an off-beat way, Tina does feel some loyalty, and she credits Ike when possible for teaching her about the business and getting her started. Ike did make her the centerpiece of one of the hottest stage shows of its time, and if it's true that he wouldn't consider using her ideas for songs,

BOB GRUEN / STAR FILE

DAVID REDFERN / RETNA

OVERLEAF: Tina kicks out, shakes and shimmies, and generally gets down, affirming her status alongside James Brown as one of pop's most explosive live performers.

Ike and Tina huddle over a microphone during one of their better moments in concert.

MICK ROCK / STAR FILE

Exuberance is the key word as Ike and Tina belt one out.

DAVID REDFERN / RETNA

A relaxed Ike seems carefree during an infrequent rest from Revue bookings.

BOB GRUEN / STAR FILE

PAUL NATKIN / STAR FILE

OPPOSITE: Outlandish costuming notwithstanding, Tina's visceral image is hardly diminished in this shot, taken during a New York concert appearance.

JOHN BELLISSIMO / RETNA

PAUL CANTY / RETNA

BOB GRUEN / STAR FILE

That million-dollar smile

LAURENS VAN HOUTEN / STAR FILE

The sexy, sultry Tina Turner demeanor

While Tina and Lionel Richie may seem stylistically mismatched, they developed a genuine rapport on-stage during his 1982 tour, for which Tina was the opening attraction.

BOB GRUEN / STAR FILE

SCOTT WEINER / RETNA

HARRISON FUNK / RETNA

it's certainly equally true that he designed the Revue and molded it around Tina as its star. Although the Ikettes' ranks from time to time included performers like P. P. Arnold, Bonnie Bramlett, and Merry Clayton, each of whom subsequently enjoyed modest success on her own, they got zippo time in the limelight, at least during the Revue's peak period.

The marriage took its toll on Tina from a performance standpoint; in later years some of her asides to audiences clearly contained a note of bitterness, a hint that things weren't quite cheery at home. The vulnerability and tenderness became excised from her voice in the early seventies

MICK ROCK

work, to be replaced by a coldness, an edge that bounced off Ike's laconic chants and fills quite well. The two looked and sounded like passing ships; there was little eye contact onstage and little rapport between them offstage. By the time the Revue had wound down to its final shows, the backstage atmosphere had become chilled—Ike's baleful glare put all on edge, and his husky voice could be heard barking orders. Tina was simply wandering around and about, as were the Ikettes.

Tina left Ike and the Revue in 1976. It was appropriate that she would leave Ike in the midst of a tour and that their final argument would take place on an airplane. The Revue had driven the length of the chitlin' circuit and crossed the ocean to rave reviews. Now things were just too far gone; Tina would just have no more of the nonsense. As she has told the

MICK ROCK

MICK ROCK

A rare tender moment on stage

PRESTON/CAMERA 5

story, "[Ike] handed me this chocolate candy, and it was melting, you know? And I was wearing a white suit and I went, 'Uh.' That's all, and he hit me. And this time I was pissed. I said, 'I'm fighting back.' "

"It's gonna work out fine . . ."

Tina left Ike with the whopping sum of thirty-six cents in her handbag. She asked for nothing when they divorced—no alimony, no child support, no community property, zero. She was alone and broke, and, as she quickly learned, liable for a bunch of blown dates previously set up for the Revue. Promoters cast a jaundiced eye at her, and venues were not so available for Tina without Ike.

To put it simply, Tina's first solo albums didn't make it. Dave Marsh, reviewing three Tina Turner solo albums from the early seventies in *The Rolling Stone Record Guide*, observed, "Without Ike Turner's grand sense of groove and melody, Tina is left on her own to shout and screech without much purpose." Tina now had to develop an act that was all her own without any heavy talent coming in off the bench to help her out.

Tina went through the rebuilding process in front of an audience that was never exactly overwhelmed by a love for black performers—Las Vegas. She appeared in the glitzy world of high-rollers and trend-setters, but she didn't get much notoriety. However, she was now free to sing whatever she pleased, so she began integrating more rock into the show, and it was her interest in Britain's pop product that led her eventually to attract the attention of English producers.

While dodging angry promoters, scrambling to make enough money to stay afloat, and hustling, Tina moved around the country as quietly as possible, fearful of Ike's possible attempts at retribution. Meanwhile she began to focus her sights on Europe. She'd had luck there before; Europe seemed to lack rigid musical expectations of her, and she was totally safe in that environment. It was during this time, while rebuilding and changing her style and approach, that Tina became cut off from the black community. No longer a steady hitmaker and not even releasing material for seven years, Tina was removed from exposure to black audiences. She's been virtually the darling of white youth ever since, a fact that must be taken into account when considering the opinions of critics who have accused her of deserting her people. She didn't; it was just the nature of the kinds of jobs and places she was booked—and welcomed—during this time.

Except for a one-time-only collaboration on the *Airwaves* album in 1978, Tina Turner bid a final farewell to Ike. She removed herself from the muck of abuse and reemerged in the spotlight as a major star. She showed him that she could survive on her own, and she showed other Doubting Thomases that perhaps Ike was not the sole fuel of the Revue.

The transformation of Anna Mae Bullock into Tina Turner had turned a seventeen-year-old girl into the pawn of a troubled but proficient musical guru. But leaving Ike and striking out on her own proved that she was psychologically able to take control of her life and career. She wasn't quite sure where she wanted to be, but coming down the road was a rendezvous with destiny that would turn Tina Turner's life around as leaving Nutbush did.

The endurance and then cessation of her marriage have shaped Tina's feelings about men, even though she hedges constantly. She stresses communication, togetherness, and equality and says her new man demonstrates these qualities. But her songs keep coming back to male imperfection. She's uneasy about men, uncomfortable with some of their misperceptions about her. If Ike did anything mentally lasting to Tina it was to destroy her innocence in a more shattering way than most marriages end the couple's illusions about each other. (This undercurrent of impatience and frustration surfaced during the performance of "What's Love Got to Do with

It" and is one more emotion that triumphant song brought forth from Tina.)

Tina was now free, but not yet totally in control. That would come later, when she hooked up with the people who would help her with the weak spots, like songwriting and production. The help would come when she tapped the resources of the British. England had been sweet once—and would prove especially sweet once more.

TERI BLOOM

CHAPTER FIVE

"River Deep, Mountain High"

Tina Turner found Las Vegas and Lake Tahoe to be different ball games. Here qualities like stage presence and routines were a bit different from the dirt-floor clubs and concert halls. Vegas was big production numbers, super-glitz, and high rollers; Tahoe was a miniature version of the same. People coming in and blowing big dollars wanted out-of-this-world entertainment. They wanted a certain detachment from the performance, with the performer transporting them to a whole new world yet maintaining a "comfortable" distance. This was nothing resembling a shared experience.

In this venue Tina began to see the importance of coordinating light shows and to recognize the pivotal place that costuming and set design played in making a performance successful. While Tina's present shows don't have the phony flavor of Vegas, she does know how to incorporate other-worldly, almost absurd costumes into her act without sacrificing grittiness. Another lesson came from singing with the Vegas pit bands. Some of the greatest musicians in the world worked in the pit bands—Martin Montgomery and James

MICK ROCK

Moody, to name just two—and like top session musicians, these guys were so sharp they could spew out cliches with minimal sweat. Yet the top singers knew how to get the pit band to wail behind them. You also had to learning pacing, refine your act to the point at which you could do it every night and breathe life into it. Tina learned her lessons well; she became a very stylized performer with a series of routines rather than merely an emotive, reacting agent who served as an illustrator of a concept.

Likewise, it was now necessary to stretch out the dancing. Tina began to get better ideas of movement—the optimum ways to maneuver around and onstage, how to achieve maximum impact when making entrances and exits. Some of these things had certainly been covered during the Revue days, but now she was a solo act; she made certain she knew everything rather than leave any details to others. Both the graceful, agile Tina of "Private Dancer" and the hip-snaking, shaking mama of "Better Be Good to Me" were refined during this period.

At one juncture, just before the success of "Let's Stay Together" hit, Tina was booked to play a series of McDonald's conventions. Given the circumstances, Tina could possibly have gotten out of the deal, but she chose to live up to her contractual commitment and play out the string. The conventions proved quite helpful. She learned that it's possible, through dedicated effort and energetic performance, to motivate even the most jaded soul. Tina's sparkling presence and majestic form proved the tonic to shake up the food company's executives. Anyway, it was the last stint she had to endure that was reminiscent of the old days.

The odyssey to England was the result of Tina's decision that Europe was the best place for a black woman who wanted to direct her primary efforts at a rock audience. She'd been popular in Britain since 1969 and hadn't forgotten the hero's welcome she'd received there. Then too, "River Deep" had hit big immediately in England and was still quite popular. She made her way to Europe in the late seventies and quickly found she was still loved and admired.

In 1979 she went on a tour of South Africa, playing only to racially mixed audiences. She did not stop to think that some might interpret her agreement to the engagement as implicitly condoning that country's *apartheid* policies. The issue was not as explosive then as now, although the United Nations had long before condemned South Africa's government-prescribed racism. The more pressing consideration for Tina was that she was in debt—heavily in debt—and this offered an opportunity to put her finances in order. Given that she was playing to mixed audiences, it may not have occurred to her that she'd ever face condemnation for her choice of venue.

TIMOTHY GREENFIELD-SANDERS

She returned from South Africa to parlay her growing European and English popularity into dollars. This came in slow stages at first, then suddenly exploded. Rod Stewart did a special satellite show broadcast across the world in 1980 and invited Tina to be his guest. (He had been impressed with her performance in one of her English concerts.) She completely obliterated Stewart with a blistering set of her own. The broadcast was the first time a new generation of music fans in America saw Tina, and what they saw was a real rocker. Here was a woman who didn't do any weeping or breast-beating about wanting her man's love and hoping she was worthy of it. She'd tell the sucker to clear out if she felt like it. Yet she didn't have the tragic/comedic blues overtones in her voice, either. She was just moving straight ahead—attacking, challenging, demanding, and inspiring. Stewart stayed a fan, too. In 1982 he and Tina recorded a duet together, "Hot Legs." It never made the charts.

Mick Jagger invited Tina to tour with the Rolling Stones in 1982. He had seen her perform several times in England and was a big fan of the Revue days. She was the first female headliner to appear onstage with them, and she garnered rave reviews.

From there Tina began reappearing on records again. Most notably, she sang on the track "Ball of Confusion" on the album *Music of Quality and Distinction*, by B.E.F., a production/subsidiary wing of the group Heaven 17; Martyn Ware and Glenn Gregory of Heaven 17 were huge fans of Tina's. With interest in her bubbling, they met to try and decide what else to record. Tina has commented many times on their meeting. "They brought me all these old R&B records, and I kept telling them, 'No, I don't want to do that.' Finally, they showed me this Al Green song. I didn't want to do that one either, but I started humming it and then said, 'Well, let's see what we can do.'" Green's version of "Let's Stay Together" was a wonderful lament. Tina turned it into a defiant com-

BOB LEAFF

Tina cavorts onstage with the Rolling Stones at the Brendan Byrne Arena in New Jersey in 1981. Mick Jagger had personally asked Tina to join the tour, and she subsequently became the first female artist to sing a duet with the Stones.

mand. Her biting opening, immediately conveying an air of bristling energy, let you know this would be no nice, pleasant love song. The song was a smash hit and caught Capitol Records by surprise. By the time they finally released the record in the United States, it hardly mattered; the song had made it to the Top 5 and had won the Silver Disc Award in England.

Tina's link with Capitol was through Britain's EMI, a sister operation. Heaven 17 was an EMI act. Capitol advanced Tina

GARY GERSHOFF/RETNA

Like a Rolling Stone

Keith Richards and David Bowie were among the many celebrities to join Tina backstage to offer their congratulations after her appearance at the Ritz in 1981.

JOHN BELLISSIMO/RETNA

GARY GERSHOFF/RETNA

Grace Jones with Tina at the Ritz, 1981

MICK ROCK

At Hammersmith Odeon, London, 1976

MICK ROCK

$150,000 and told her they wanted an album. *Private Dancer* was done in two weeks in the spring of 1984, shortly before the Lionel Richie tour. Rupert Hine, producer for the band called Fixx, contributed the song "I Might Have Been Queen," and Mark Knopfler, of Dire Straits and supersessionist fame, gave her "Private Dancer," which had been slated for a Dire Straits album. Terry Britton of Heaven 17 donated "What's Love Got to Do with It," the song that ultimately catapulted the album to the top of the charts.

One can advance many reasons why English songwriters have given Tina her hits. One notion is that the English have no hangups about a black woman doing so-called male music; another says that they're in tune with Tina because they view her in a totally different light—they really see her as the powerful, assertive individual she wants to be and therefore select and write material to fit that image. Perhaps the real truth is that England loved Tina from the beginning, has

GARY GERSHOFF/RETNA

With Susan Sarandon at the Ritz, 1981

ALAIN MINGAM/GAMMA LIAISON

Tina was a triumph at the Pavilion in Paris in 1978, marking one of her most acclaimed concerts since leaving Ike a few years before.

always been more conscious of her potential, and welcomed her experiments and desire to move beyond playing the part of Ike's foil. The notion that the English are simply better songwriters than the Americans, just doesn't wash, but they are more attuned to the kind of lyrics and arrangements that Tina prefers. Her music is a crazy mix of slightly out-of-date backings and rather advanced theories. She has not shown any interest in the current developments in black music; go-go, rap, and electro-funk don't seem appropriate to what Tina wants, and it's doubtful that her style would allow her to share space with the barrage of technology that imbues the HI-NRG format. She likes the white noise/distorted guitar riffing

CURT GUNTHER/CAMERA 5

backgrounds, a style that currently seems on the wane in America. English trends tend to be behind America anyhow, and right now Tina's music consciously goes against the grain, at least in terms of a lot of what's on the charts.

Tina's participation in the Lionel Richie tour was at Richie's direct request. He was impressed with her cover of "Let's Stay Together" and wanted someone on his bill who had something currently out. Tina admits to initial uncertainty. "Before the tour I was nervous because Lionel Richie's crowd isn't necessarily my crowd. They're an older crowd, but after the tour started, I found they appreciated my music."

GARY GERSHOFF/RETNA

After her opening at the Ritz, Tiny Tim told Tina, "I wish I could hit some of your low notes."

KEN SEIDENSTEIN

From left: Mary Tyler Moore, Tina, Diana Ross, and Iman

Tina more or less was her own manager for a long time. In 1981, Lee Kramer, then the manager of Olivia Newton-John, became her manager, and when he dropped out, his assistant, Roger Davies, took over. The greatest thing Davies has done has been to keep Tina before the media, yet in a way that doesn't overexpose her or make her look like a huckster. The spate of interviews after the 1985 broadcasts of the American Music Awards, Grammies, and American Video Awards for 1984 always focused on a cool, calm, and articulate Tina Turner. Sometimes she appeared as the congenial relic baffled by her new-found success. At other times she was the saucy lady on top and proud of it. It was masterful use of media, and Davies deserves credit for making sure she stayed on the case.

For Americans, there are down sides to Tina Turner's being the darling of the English, namely the fact that she plans to record her next album there. Secondly, she's not interacting with the movers and shakers of the creative community in the United States. Granted, there's no obligation on Tina's part to do this, and there's little chance that an American could write or produce anything for her properly. But it would be interesting to see what an Ashford and Simpson—or Bernard Edwards, Kashif, or a host of others—might come up with for her. But the British stuck with Tina during a time when she was forgotten elsewhere, and they've demonstrated that right now, at least, they're on the same creative wavelength.

The England/Tina question could be viewed as the pop extension of Europe supporting jazz greats while Americans yawn and flip on Top 40 radio stations like Z-100. There's no simple answer; black and white pop in America is very hit oriented, and audiences do tend toward memory lapses for any act that goes a year without releasing a record. Then again, there are other artists who keep going without constant hits or contracts. (James Brown is a prime current example.) No, in this case there's just a special love, a special empathy that's made England a mecca for Tina Turner and English songwriters the best people to put her voice to its maximum use on vinyl.

With the enormous success of *Private Dancer* and the huge outgrowth of support for Tina in America, there is no doubt that Tina will eventually come home. That may be a chauvinistic attitude, but it does appear likely nonetheless. It seems likely, too, that Tina will continue to make inroads into the black community, particularly the southern black community—which is not to say that she's lost sight of her people or that she doesn't retain an identification with Nutbush. But the continued identification with England and worldwide fame may result in a "crossover" label and thereby appear to place her beyond the reach of the black media and community. Fortunately, it hasn't happened yet, and Tina seems inclined to prevent it.

EBET ROBERTS

CHAPTER SIX

"Working Together"

If any song ever served to propel a career, then "What's Love Got to Do with It" has been the force that catapulted Tina Turner into the pop stratosphere. Her vocal performance on that record established indelibly her coming of age as a singer. She paced herself through the stanzas, letting each one stand as its own vehicle and yet linking them through a shattering, jagged reading of the choruses, hooks, and repeated phrases.

The song's opening lines establish an aura of pensiveness; she poses the question juxtaposed with a challenge, immediately throwing you off-balance as you ponder just what she's saying. After detailing her reactions and feelings, she throws a loop by saying that her response to seemingly romantic stimuli not only has nothing to do with love but may not necessarily be romantic or positive. The song's mood has shifted from one of anticipation to one of aggravation, and Tina's shimmering and declarative tone and delivery are now raising listener reaction to a frenzied state. She continues the pattern throughout of raising and then muting the moods;

sometimes she sounds a note of aggressiveness, at other times a tone of puzzlement.

"What's Love Got to Do with It" never resolves fully the issue of love versus lust, and that's part of its strength, as well as the emotional tour-de-force turned in by Tina. That's also demonstrated in the adoption of a breezy, reggae-inflected arrangement. The music sways, bends, and seems to weave around Tina's lines rather than become subservient to her lead. The rhythm gives her enough latitude to vary her approach and alter her style often; and the flowing structure provides space for fine instrumental interludes that don't draw too much attention to themselves but still help flesh out the number. The loping, lingering harmonica solo that comes midway through the break is a perfect example. You hear a masterful solo with elements of blues phrasing and timbre that fades out just when it should, rather than drone on and get stepped on.

Lyrically the song may not be quite as revolutionary as some critics have suggested. Tina's sentiments may not be the standard love-at-all-costs sop that usually oozes out of love songs, but she's not exactly closing the door on it, either. While she does make a case for love's negative qualities, the wavering aspects of the lyrics seem to indicate less of a hardening and more of a reflective framework in terms of her emotional outlook.

"When I first heard the song, I thought it was a cute little song, nothing special, just a cute bit of music. I'm sure glad I was mistaken," Tina said during an interview that aired as part of the syndicated radio series "Special Edition" early in 1985. She's echoed this notion in many other interviews. It's clear she saw nothing special in the song at first but was bowled over by its widespread commercial potential. The song was a Number One hit on the black charts, the pop charts, and the dance charts, and helped lift the *Private Dancer* LP to the top of the pop lists in every trade publication.

SL/RETNA

EBET ROBERTS

A steamy performance in 1983

The video of "What's Love Got to Do with It" expresses the song's ambivalence even more sharply. Tina, dressed in a blue jacket and a miniskirt that showcases her incredible legs, ambles through a Greenwich Village neighborhood. She constantly comes across situations that seem perfect examples of love in place: a couple engaged in deep conversation or a child playing. Her angular strides and very impassioned portrait put the song into another element. Now you can see the anguish on her face, witness the tension she displays when singing the chorus, and watch her skitter and gracefully move to the beat, showing off a sexuality miles apart from the burlesque show routines of the Revue. Tina seems vulnerable, desirable, troubled, and engaging all in the same time frame. With her teased mane of hair giving her the regal splendor of royalty, and the quivering, compelling inflections she's providing in her singing keeping your attention riveted to the video, "What's Love Got to Do with It" becomes a true musical/visual masterpiece, as magnificent an example of music video's potential excellence as Michael Jackson's "Thriller" and "Billie Jean," without the megabucks production touches and corps of recruited actors to boot.

"What's Love Got to Do with It" can also be deemed the real start of the Tina Turner boom period. Since that song's astronomical success, Tina has become *the* woman for the eighties. She was selected as one of *McCall's*' most physically attractive women of the year 1984, and her advertisement for that magazine featured her face in a full-page spread that was later incorporated as part of a television production. She's slated to appear in the third Mad Max film in 1985, and her name appears in gossip publications from the *National Enquirer* to *Rolling Stone*'s celebrity spread. She appears regularly now on TV's "Entertainment Tonight"; her every appearance at a party or public gathering is deemed worthy of two or three minutes of airtime.

"What's Love Got to Do with It" stands the test of time.

CHRIS WALTER/RETNA

"Bold soul sister . . ."

ANDREA LAUBACH/RETNA

The black leather jacket makes one of its first appearances in 1984.

KENNETH KATZ/STAR FILE

MICK ROCK

Despite the fact that it could be heard about one hundred times a day at its peak and that the video has been aired at least that often, there are new aspects of Tina's performance to be discovered with each listen, and the video never ceases to enthrall. Tina presented such a multidimensional portrait and sang splendidly enough to ensure that when historians and critics of a later era evaluate the complete Tina Turner discography, "What's Love Got to Do with It" will rank supreme in their view.

Yet I'm troubled by the song, most notably by its implied theme of the failed nature of love. Certainly Tina's life experiences would naturally lead her to express a bittersweet view of romance, and it is a refreshing change to hear a woman challenge long-held assertions about love without resorting to rhetoric or just taking the revenge tack. But there's a beauty within Tina that the song does not completely reveal; in fact, no song since the early days has ever been able to tap her tender side completely. Tina does reveal a vulnerability, but you don't hear the sweetness that once was displayed in her delivery. Perhaps the song's nature made it impossible to interject this emotional aspect, but it's the one element that seems to be missing from an otherwise unforgettable rendition.

While the complete *Private Dancer* album stands as one of 1984's greatest musical moments, nothing Tina ever does will surpass "What's Love Got to Do with It." It takes its place alongside a handful of masterpieces that lay open the inequalities and burdens of love and then leave them unresolved for us to tackle.

BRIAN ARIS/OUTLINE

CHAPTER SEVEN

"Honky-Tonk Woman"

The first time Tina Turner took the stage as a featured member of the Ike and Tina Turner Revue, she proved that she possessed incredible energy, maddening sexual electricity, and the physical charisma to mesmerize, tantalize, and inflame the passions of her audience. But by restructuring her image, she's moved far beyond her days as a bump-and-grind hoofer. Her dance routines, onstage movements, and total stage presence are as magnetic as any single performer since a youthful James Brown or Little Richard, and she's merged seemingly contradictory postures so seamlessly that any single interpretation of Tina live can be questioned or defended with equal facility. She summons up at various times her blues-queen-in-suffering guise, her liberated-woman pose, her wavering beauty caught in the throes of romantic indecision, her I'm-just-one-of-you empathy bit, and her let's-just-rock-the-night-away role. And none of these are accomplished with the cynicism with which the press is likely to describe them.

The delicate juxtaposition of multiple images has done several things for Tina. It's made her likable and even idolized among hard-line feminists, who have always been uncomfortable with the stereotyped pop music portrait of a love-starved female; it's given her a sympathetic reading among the gay population, which tends to adore artists who don't seem completely certain about the pluses and minuses of romantic entanglements; and it's connected her with nu-

Proud Mary

BOB LEAFE/STAR FILE

merous heterosexual male fans who enjoy the freedom to speculate and conjure up their own images and perceptions of what Tina Turner may or may not be like.

No matter how much Tina may proclaim she's just a homebody, the photograph of her clad in classic male turn-on costume of black shirt and sitting with her legs lingering invitingly on the album cover of *Private Dancer* sets off thoughts of magic moments. She seems to have caught onto the downside of this image; the cover of her 1985 single "Show Some Respect" features her clothed in something that at least covers her entire body, although the use of a feathery fabric may ultimately trigger the same reaction.

But of all the things most responsible for Tina Turner's widespread magnetism, her dancing remains the most important. On some levels, she hardly matches the talents of some of her contemporaries. Patti Labelle, for instance, can swoop, whip, and move across a stage faster and in more unorthodox ways than Tina can, while some of the dance music/disco rockers, like Shannon, seem to conduct dance and rhythm seminars as they perform. Today Tina doesn't seem to have the command of her dance moves the way she did in the Revue days. Back then she could lead the Ikettes in high-step routines that surpassed anything to be seen at Radio City or in Las Vegas.

What Tina does do is merge graceful extrapolation with gymnastic agility; she can weave and bob or leap and flip, depending on what's called for. The videos of "What's Love Got to Do with It" and "Private Dancer" exemplify the two extremes of her graceful motif. Her walk down the street on "What's Love Got to Do with It" is graceful, angular, striking. Her turns catch your attention, and the strides hold it. It's the kind of walk that begs for some Hollywood flack in the background yelling, "What a walk! What a stride!"

DEE TOSA/RETNA

DEE TOSA/RETNA

No impressive costumes or skimpy outfit can punctuate Tina's message more clearly than her resilient spirit and powerful voice.

BOB LEAFE/STAR FILE

Her "Private Dancer" entrance is mysterious and inviting but intriguing as well. Here she moves at a pace that is neither slow nor quick; perfectly timed stops and pauses hold the tension as you wait and wonder what will happen when she reaches her destination.

The great thing about these moments is that neither is explicitly sexual by design; some people may even view them as asexual. But Tina's physical movements alone give them an attractiveness, an alluring quality that no other individual could have communicated in the same situation.

While the subject of male fantasies is an easily negotiable one, it is pivotal to understanding the Tina Turner magic. Her movements and dancing arouse more than just a lustful reaction. Getting that reaction may be the initial motivation, but mixed in with that come feelings of apprehension, wonderment, excitement, and even dismay. I can think of no other major female star of whom I've heard so many men say, "She scares me" or "Man, I'm not sure I could handle her, but I'd sure like to try." Watching Tina at work in her various roles, one is transported through a range of emotions, and you wind up not being real clear about anything except the fact that you've been captivated.

It seems clear that black and white men have different feelings—and fantasies—about Tina. Black males' reactions seem to span the gamut from complete fluster to total awe, from those who'd like an interlude and nothing more to those displeased at a perspective they view as not completely cognizant of the black community. Some such comments were in fact aired by males on New York radio station WLIB-AM the day after Tina's Image award nomination was withdrawn by the Hollywood NAACP because of her South African sojourn. (The award is given to artists the NAACP feels have done the most to convey a positive image for blacks.) Callers were expressing sentiments like, "Tina Turner's been hanging around them white folk so long she's starting to think like

DEE TOSA/RETNA

Tina's grinding ballads eventually came to play second fiddle to the churning rockers that she now proclaims as her life's blood.

them," or "Some people will do anything for money." However, so far this has remained the sentiment of only a small portion of the populace, although the fact that it seems centered among the more activist wing of the black community may be grounds for concern to Tina's public relations people.

The striking, statuesque body of Tina Turner certainly triggers a large number of male fantasies. This is one area where changing sexual notions and public behavioral patterns have asserted themselves. Anyone who saw the Revue

Sexy Ida

DAVID REDFERN/RETNA

in its earlier days can attest that in the beginning Tina and company wore a lot more clothes than they did later on. On the steamy T.A.M.I. video, for instance, Tina and the Ikettes are fully clothed, which caused one fan to comment, "God, I've never seen her with that many clothes on."

Her eyes are magnificent; she can give you the look of a temptress, a fallen angel, a weary traveler, or an angry protestor without coming off the least bit phony. Her poses have made each album cover or single photo an exercise in pictorial splendor. But the vaunted Tina Turner legs are arguably her most attention-grabbing asset; they've become her signature as incontestably as Liberace's candelabra or Little Richard's hair are those artists' signatures. No one's better suited for the return of the miniskirt; she knows that her legs have become public property and it makes her proud. At the 1984 American Video awards (broadcast early in 1985), when giving her tribute to James Brown, who was receiving the Hall of Fame Award, Tina told Rod Stewart, on the video screen via satellite connection, that she wished she could give him a hand in person, then changed it to "give you a leg." It's also notable that Tina's concerts become most energized when she begins her shaking, whirling, segments, legs flaring, whipping, and strutting around the stage and her wild mane flying. She completely milks the routine.

But there are clearly negative aspects to this leg fascination. Most fundamental is the reduction of flesh-and-blood woman to limbs and joints in the worst porno mag fashion. It's a point that Tina addresses in all of her interviews, confiding that she does not always fling her legs around when she's at home, or dress in miniskirts. Perhaps the subject of Tina Turner's legs has been overemphasized, and yet, they are so much a part of her attraction. It's more than just observing an element of the woman's sexuality. It's also finding oneself drawn into the image, and so forcefully that it becomes disturbing.

Tina and her backup singers rip it up during a New York performance shortly after "Let's Stay Together" hit it big on both sides of the Atlantic in 1984.

Confessional soul at its best

SIMON FOWLER/RETNA

PAUL CANTY/RETNA

Plumage adds to the visual impact.

Intimacy and rapport are the two major attributes of any Tina Turner concert. No matter how elaborate the costumes are or how intricate the dance routines, Tina's concerts strive for the church feeling of the Revue days. Sometimes this is achieved by letting audience members come on stage and participate in the show; other times Tina and a guitarist or keyboardist will begin dancing and exchanging quips. But she never lets a sense of separation creep up between herself and her audience, and she needs no flashy gimmicks to accomplish the intimacy. Tina conducts her shows like tours of her private home; she guides the audience through numbers, talks about how much a song means to her or why she chose to use it, and periodically checks to see if the folks are happy. Much of this is standard concert conduct and nothing that Tina invented, but her ability to speak directly and with a clear sincerity makes concert audiences feel a oneness with their idol.

Tina's shows, image, and personality have not yet reached the point where boredom has caused a jaded star to emerge. At the Grammies and the American Music Awards for 1984 she was radiant, projecting a happiness at receiving awards that struck observers as both real and truly heartwarming. The sense of humility, the quality of undiluted innocence were on display for a nationwide viewing public, making fans of them all, even if just for the moment. And the next morning, when the taped interviews rolled on "Good Morning America" and "The Today Show," Tina once again was magnificent. She repeatedly answered the same stupid questions over and over (How did she feel? Wasn't it great to win these awards? How did it feel to be recognized?) with grace and pride.

It is this deeply rooted graciousness, this earnest desire to please people and retain the simple, humble traits of her upbringing, that are the real strengths of Tina Turner. It's a tribute to her brilliance as an artistic performer that she's

GARY GERSHOFF/RETNA

managed to become a superstar by capably working and molding a fantasy image and a series of perceptions so far from the way in which she'd prefer to be viewed. She's been able to appeal to the darkest side of male sexual urges without becoming publicly bitter about it; she's gradually become one of the most visible spokespersons for the rights of women in relationships without having to parrot politically "with-it" rhetoric or anguish over her professional and personal status. Finally, she has given us a body of dance and physical performances rich in visual improvisation, earthy enough to conjure up memories of the blues and hard times, graceful enough to make us gasp in wonder. She has emphatically shown us the difference between talented dancing and dancing with talent.

DAVID REDFERN/RETNA

CHAPTER EIGHT

"Proud Mary"

Contradictions arise repeatedly when one examines closely the gap between Tina Turner as perceived by both her fans and society as a whole and the goals and aspirations espoused by Tina offstage and in interviews. She views herself as a very reserved, deeply religious individual who believes among other things that she was on earth previously as a French dancer. She takes time, before and after concerts, to chant and practice the tenets of her Buddhist faith. Yet her Baptist background probably accounts just as much as her current religion for the uneasiness and continual image correcting that she seems to include whenever she talks about herself.

She told Britain's *Daily Mirror* that she ardently dislikes the feeling implicit in her act that she's not quite the embodiment of chastity. "I'm a very moral person. People seem to think you can't sing rock and roll the way I do and still be a lady." However, that wish to be perceived as something other than a sexually permissive, loose woman clashes head-on into an onstage personality that Tina herself has carefully cultivated and in which she revels and takes pride in maintaining. "I don't want to beg and plead and weep and moan anymore," Tina said in a March 1985 *Newsweek* story. "I've had enough of that. Now what I like to sing are ass-kicking songs. I want to get crazy. That's who I am."

It's the clash between the public perception and private reality that enables her to be so convincing when doing a song like "Private Dancer." While in one sense her struggle is just one more chronicle in the long battle between the flesh and the devil, which has been a foundation of contemporary music, it's much more significant because she neither feels nor expresses any guilt about the gap between the things she truly believes and what she lets people imagine, nor has she altered her behavior to match the audience's expectations.

BOB LEAFE

Some routine finger-popping, plus the usual fireworks

She doesn't smoke, seldom drinks, and has a fierce disdain for any type of drugs, a repulsion cultivated by years of watching Ike's overindulgence. But she doesn't use the platform of superstardom to proselytize for her religion either. She speaks frankly and openly about it and her belief in reincarnation only as a part of the overall Tina Turner profile; it's neither the most important nor least important thing in her life.

Tina Turner's embrace of rock is not something she conveniently adopted; she truly loves and admires this music. Some of her thoughts and notions about traditional black music cause consternation in the ranks when she expresses them, but she has not hedged on her feelings. If anything, she's now even more of a rock advocate than she was in the past. "I never wanted to sing and scream and do all that wailing, but's that how I was produced in the early days by my ex-husband," Tina said in the *Newsweek* story. "I realized I liked the way people like Eric Clapton and the Rolling Stones had mixed white and black music, taking feelings from black people and adding it to their own. Blues to me is depressing. White music has a liberating feeling about it, and I needed a change."

No doubt these sentiments grate on the sensibilities of blues and soul fans. But whether you buy them or not, understanding that these feelings govern Tina Turner's selection of music, tailoring of routines, and choice of producers and session mates is critical to understanding that Tina views herself first and foremost as a rock singer—not a black singer who does rock or even a black rock singer, but strictly a *rock singer*. She feels that she's always wanted to do this music and that the material done since 1984 represents her finest vocal efforts.

But Caroline Sullivan, of *Melody Maker* magazine, reviewing Tina's March 1985 tour appearance in London's Wembley Arena, complained, "Tina turned up all the way, falls victim to the rampant rockism of her voice and to an apparently

In Michigan, 1984

uncontrollable urge to barrel aside the dual deadweights of nuance and cadence. 'Soul,' whatever that means, isn't in it. . . . She's left careening down the American AOR path ('Show Some Respect' and 'Steel Claw'), and so it goes tonight. For every shockingly gorgeous 'Let's Stay Together' . . . there are two like 'I Might Have Been Queen,' all guitars a la squeal, and just busting out of their leather pedalpushers."

Her major career objectives revolve around keeping her position as preeminent rock queen. She's justifiably proud of what's she achieved and scoffs at any notion that age may soon begin having a telling effect on her live performance. She admitted to being forty-four in 1985 and has often commented, "I've had my kids and I'm still in pretty good shape, ain't I?" to quick choruses of agreement. It's a sign of her ambition that she lists as a prime goal the desire to be the reigning rock money earner on the female side. "I want to be the first black rock woman to fill a football stadium," Tina said right after the Grammy Awards for 1984. "Janis Joplin did it for the white girls, and I want to do it for the black." Despite her refusal to be depicted principally as a black singer, Tina has been one of the most cooperative and featured crossover acts in the black press (or at least she was until the furor over the 1979 South African concerts erupted in 1984). She has been featured repeatedly in *Jet* magazine and was the cover subject for *Ebony* magazine's May 1985 issue. Sporadic criticism notwithstanding, quotes from Tina appear more frequently in mainstream black publications than virtually any other major black act with a principally pop-rock constituency.

Tina's frankness is not confined to the music or spiritual arena. She has no illusions about her looks and sized herself up this way in *Rolling Stone* (2/14/85): "You can't put me down with the ugly ones and you can't put me up with the pretty ones. . . . I'm in the middle lane." She freely admits that she hated the way she looked when she was young and has described herself often as having had a short torso and

MICHAEL PUTLAND/RETNA

neck and being all legs. She has not yet leaped into the world of celebrity exercise tips, but she does stress diet and appearance as part of the total package. She no longer eats much red meat, despite the soul food heritage of west Tennessee, and she has sworn off starches and fats. She uses makeup only on stage and gives twenty-five years of performing and walking in airports as the reason for her wondrous shape. At five-feet-four-inches and 126 pounds, she is aided considerably in photos and on album covers by retouching and in televised appearances by the additive nature of the camera. She isn't quite as robust or physically towering as one might expect, though she hardly could be called out-of-shape. The flowering, circling hair that's become as much her trademark as the long legs is the product of nothing complicated or exacting. Tina says she simply washes it and has pieces of other hair woven into her own, though the bulk of what you see belongs to her. She calls the look "natural," while others have labeled it everything from "messy" to inspired and chic.

Tina may be unparallelled as a star who's been able to keep her family and friends out of the limelight. Her two sons Craig, twenty-six, and Ronnie, twenty-four, are known only to avid researchers and fans. Tina avoids any questions aimed at deciphering the identity of the person she calls "her special friend" and only offers for public consumption the fact that he's different from her other lovers in that he's strong, financially secure, and emotionally able to handle her lifestyle and the long periods of separation it requires. When asked to discuss her relationship with her family, Tina is once again frank yet succinct.

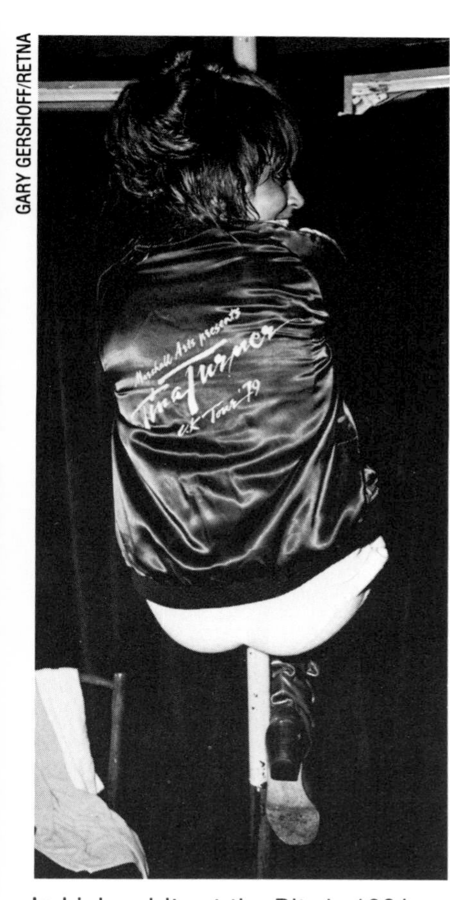

GARY GERSHOFF/RETNA

In high spirits at the Ritz in 1981

"We're close, but I'm not mother, mother, munch, munchy," Tina says in describing her feelings about her sons. "I'm not that mother figure. I've never been real conscious of age, because of my lifestyle—rock and roll music, traveling, always surrounded by young people. So you don't get stuck in that old family raising and school and CPA's and all that. . . . Oh, no . . . what is it? . . . PTA." While those words don't especially depict her as a candidate for mother of the year, they do speak to the quality that Tina Turner cites as most essential—her freedom.

She has always valued freedom above all else—freedom to sing and do what she pleases, freedom to achieve, and even freedom to fail if the circumstances merit that. Such ventures as her country LP in the early seventies and her role in the film *Tommy* seem prime examples of her urge to present herself as capable of the unexpected; certainly her view of white music as a liberating force is the most appealing aspect of rock for her purposes. The pride that she felt and expressed after winning three Grammys at least partly goes back to the fact that she won them on her own, free of Ike. "A year ago I took away all of my achievements from when Ike

and I were together and put them on a separate wall, and I left a wall in my music room free. And I said to myself, 'All right, you're alone. I'm going to see what I'm going to do.' A year later that wall is full of silver and platinum—triple platinum for one album."

The one area in which Tina has failed to venture thus far has been songwriting, and that may leave her open to criticism as a performer. She is not the multifaceted, conceptual artist that a Prince or Michael Jackson is and thus must still be ranked slightly beneath them. *Private Dancer* may be as great a record as *Purple Rain*, but Prince composed the latter and even turned it into a major film. Tina's wise enough to know that at some future point she must consider songwriting, but her interpretive powers have thus far been capable of filling the void. She describes her method of operation here as "changing the rules to do what I wanna do," but it's hard not to fantasize about what would happen if Tina made up her own rules.

Tina can and does make her own rules within the cinematic landscape. Her first entry into it, her appearance as the Acid Queen in *Tommy*, was erratic and even campy but still memorable. Her next, a major role in *Mad Max 3*, the latest in the series of Mel Gibson thriller/allegories/satires, has been eagerly awaited, and Tina says she's spending much of her little free time reading potential scripts. She has a preference for action roles and says she doesn't want "to do sexy movies. And I'm not funny, so I couldn't do comedy. I want to be dealing with some kind of war. Physical strength in a woman—that's what I am."

There is a constant maze of contradictions seeping through every part of Tina's life, and it extends to her memories of the past. In one account she describes in detail horrible beatings, tales of mental domination, and chronicles of immense drug

MICK ROCK

abuse, yet in another she behaves as if her past was just a mild interlude before striking paydirt. "I didn't really have any bad times," Tina told *People* magazine when she was featured in the 1984 year-end issue, which listed her as one of the most intriguing personalities of the year. "It looked like bad times from the orthodox way of thinking, but the times without a record have been great for me." She shrugs off the eight years she spent on the supper club/cabaret circuit as just a part of her life that she had to experience in order to build a reputation as a solo act, and she won't even badmouth the lengthy stint she had to suffer appearing at McDonald's conventions just before "Let's Stay Together" broke big.

EBET ROBERTS

In New York, 1983

ROBIN KAPLAN/RETNA

Tina reaches for a high note during a 1983 performance.

The tension between the Tina Turner we see and the real Tina Turner, together with her brilliant abilities as a performer and a razor-sharp media sense, are all responsible for her current status. She has been able to resolve the seeming contradiction between being the embodiment of sexual ardor in performance and her goal of living a simple, upright, normal existence, and she's taken charge of her professional image without having to assume an overly assertive public stance. She credits Heaven 17 musicians Martyn Ware and Dire Straits' Glenn Gregory and Mark Knopfler, each of whom contributed material to *Private Dancer,* with pivotal roles in her success; she's had no hesitancy about welcoming big-name musicians onto the stage to sing with her during concerts. While she talks about "attempting to find the balance of equality between men and women" on the one hand, she also talks about sharing, about having to be with someone who knows how to communicate, how to share things, and who wants to be a partner rather than a slave or a master.

SUZI GIBBONS

MICHAEL PUTLAND/RETNA

Tina tells the crowd just what it'll take to satisfy her.

Tina Turner has an ultimate mission beyond just the immediate goals of continued musical growth and film stardom. She sees herself having a genuine impact culturally, and views the media clout she now enjoys as critical to maintaining her stance and visibility once the current hype fades.

"I'm gonna focus on this. I think that's gonna be my message, that's why I'm here, and I think that's why I'm gonna be as powerful as I am. Because in order to get people to listen to you, you've got to be some kind of landmark, some kind of foundation. You don't listen to people that don't mean anything to you. You have to have something there to make people believe you. And so I think that's what's going on now. I'm getting their attention now, and then when I'm ready they'll listen. And they'll hear."

NEAL PRESTON/CAMERA 5

CHAPTER NINE

"What's Love Got to Do with It?"

Tina Turner occupies a position within the American cultural pantheon that twenty years ago would be deemed unattainable for any black performer, male or female. When the Revue was making its finest records and giving outrageously hypnotic concerts, few people envisioned or considered a life for Tina outside the purview of Ike and the Revue. The erratic, feeble quality of her solo projects in the seventies seemed to suggest that Ike's musical domination of her talents may have been her only ticket to success. But she's made a drastic turnaround and accomplished unprecedented success essentially on the strength of a handful of great singles packaged into one great album. There's been no steady progression, no slow, block-by-block career building; instead, she's leaped from the edge of oblivion to the peak of mass acceptance.

Tina Turner's musical and physical gifts, while considerable, are not overpowering in comparison with those of several of her contemporaries. Her voice doesn't have the chilling quality of Aretha Franklin's or the awesome range and clarity

Tina enjoys the luxuries that the 1980s afford her.

A. J. PANTSIOS/STAR FILE

ANDREA LAUBACH/RETNA

of Chaka Khan's. Tina's a strikingly beautiful woman, but her sensuality must be presented in its most advantageous context for maximum impact. When you see photographs of Tina at home in her favorite apparel of jeans and floppy, smudged shirt, your reaction isn't the one you'd have if you saw Jayne Kennedy pruning roses in the yard. Yet Tina gets selected in polls for best hairstyle, most physically striking, most admired, etc., and her every public entry and exit is observed, evaluated, and anticipated.

She's become the ultimate crossover artist, moving from one musical genre to another—and thus aiming for a new audience—without being crossed out; she's never made any effort to blunt or soft-pedal her blackness, even though she's loudly maintained that she's a rocker and not a soul/R&B stylist. But whether Tina sings the Motels' "Total Control" or Ann Peebles' "I Can't Stand the Rain," you can still hear the smears, the quirks, and gutbucket sensibility seeping through. Her stage shows may be highly polished, patterned affairs with multiple costume changes, high-tech sound, designed sets, and flamboyant lighting, but Tina still works the audience and draws from it a loving, cathartic reaction only a master could generate. She's a role model for every constituency, from divorced women inspired by her resiliency to youthful dancers amazed by her tirelessness and agility.

She projects a confidence, a certainty about who she is and what she wants that belies the air of mysticism that swirls around Prince and the sense of caged adolescence that makes Michael Jackson at times seem like a visitor from another planet. She's even survived some questionable decisions and emerged with her popularity intact. She was neither comfortable nor completely welcomed by audiences when she toured with Lionel Richie in 1983. Richie's crowds react to a romanticism far different from Tina's eroticism; they desire gushy tributes and warm praises rather than aggressive salutations and confrontational poses. Yet Tina and Richie managed to work together without incident (at least none that surfaced in print), and they even performed together during some of the stops.

The only major public relations blunder Tina has made was her trip to South Africa, which she took before ascending to the top of mass consciousness. Her lack of sensitivity to the feelings that could raise as much as five years later made her vulnerable to charges from black nationalists that her bid for glory was causing her to turn her back on the struggles of her people. Wisely, she belatedly issued an apology, taking full blame for the error and speaking frankly about her past ignorance of the overall South African issue and the ramifications of her appearance. She later participated in the "USA for Africa" project, in which her short solo easily ranks as one of the more memorable on the "We Are the World" single. These moves signal both a sharp sense of the need not to burn bridges within the black community and a commitment to the audiences that supported her long before she ever became a name act as a solo performer.

But Tina's status inspires more black pride than several other folks one might name. She's soft-spoken but very articulate and direct during interviews; there's none of the silly self-consciousness or star mannerisms in her television appearances. She simply sits and reacts to questions in a casual, what's-the-big-deal fashion, and she enjoys herself and projects this to the viewer. Likewise her videos have avoided the typical garish scenarios; and they have placed her in imaginative, unorthodox, or surprising situations that really are linked to the lyrics of the songs they visually outline. From "Let's Stay Together," with its whirling montage of Tina and two women performing alluring and electrifying movements to "Private Dancer" 's depression-era set and gangster costumes, Tina's videos have established her as an artist capable of using the video medium for self-expression rather than momentary attention-grabbing.

Private Dancer will ultimately rank alongside Marvin Gaye's *What's Going On*, Stevie Wonder's *Innervisions*, and Smokey Robinson's *A Quiet Storm* in its importance as a concept album and statement. Tina's scope extends across the spectrum of love and illuminates all its defects and sores. It celebrates the ambivalence of sexual attraction, asserts the right of a woman to demand and expect respect, and then concludes by exposing the seamy side of impersonal relationships and the toll they take on everyone involved. She also puts to rest, if there was still doubt, the issue of whether a black artist can function in an ostensibly white idiom. *Private Dancer* may have a black base and black influences, but it's a rock album overall. Tina doesn't sing the blues or search for salvation, she rears up and cuts loose. She also disproves the canard that women can't really rock; she may not play the guitar, but she certainly sustains her energy and power throughout the album.

There's no visible reason for Tina not to be able to maintain her megastar status for at least the rest of the decade, barring any other public relations disasters. Reports of her forty-city European tour in the spring of 1985 indicate no slowing down or coasting in her stage shows.

Musically, her material has remained extremely high. Her newest single, "Show Some Respect," issued in April 1985, conveys the same bristling spirit as "Better Be Good to Me," while the flip side, a cover of Prince's "Let's Pretend We're Married," actually surpasses the original for saucy impact and sensual vitality. Her acting career seems ready to take off, with the upcoming appearance in *Mad Max 3* probably destined to cause as much commotion as her frenetic, wild-eyed portrayal in *Tommy* did in the early seventies. Add to all this the constant media obsession with her family life (which

Tina relaxes off stage in the outfit she prefers: jeans, T-shirt, and very little makeup.

LISA SEIFERT/STAR FILE

she keeps very hidden and private) and romantic attachments and you have the ingredients for extended celebrity status.

Often when I see Tina on the tube or hear her wailing on the radio I think back to a time twenty years ago, when her audiences were all black, her venues were clubs and buildings southern cities were glad to let stand in disrepair until they crumbled, and the only radio stations that aired her music were 1000-watt daytimers with directional antennas that went off at sundown. A twelve-year-old kid with a love of music that his parents insisted did nothing but keep his people in mental slavery curled up with Tina's music at night, when WLAC could be heard on a beat-up radio, and sneaked in to see her live whenever possible. He marveled at her grace, idolized her voice, and wondered if someday he'd see her someplace other than a dreary town slowly climbing out of stone-age segregation.

Now she's on magazine covers, plays every major club in New York City, and is the adopted queen of American pop. While I laud her success and still marvel at her talent, a troubling feeling nags at me. Tina Turner doesn't belong to the people at the VIP Club or the Paradise anymore; in a sense, she's outgrown that existence like so many others. In many ways the chitlin' circuit hurt as many careers as it helped; performers grew embittered at working for peanuts and fled the business, or frustrations erupted and concerts concluded in a rush with hasty retreats to the door to avoid injury.

Tina most likely remembers those clubs and the walks alongside the edge of the stage to shake the hands of fans. And there's still the same urgency and excitement in her voice when she sings "Let's Stay Together" that were there when she and Ike sang about "Hard Times." The only thing missing is the tentativeness, the holding back and waiting for the signal to accelerate. Tina Turner now gives the signals and calls the shots. Ike and the extra-long guitar cord are gone; so are the horn section and the Ikettes. Only Tina remains: bigger, more beautiful, and more loved than ever before. Her time has come.

AARON RAPPAPORT

CHAPTER TEN

"Reflections"

As of this writing, Tina Turner is finishing up a European tour, awaiting the release of the movie *Mad Max 3*, which presents her in a featured role, and anticipating both the release of the follow-up to *Private Dancer* and a triumphant tour of America. Her self-confidence is evident. And her penchant for saying what she feels yielded this gem in comments made to *USA Today* in March 1985 about her participation in the "USA for Africa" project: "Well, although the song was written by two blacks, it was the performances of the white singers that really brought it to life." Typically, there was little fallout from Tina's comments; she remains the darling of audiences virtually across the board.

The only hard question concerning Tina Turner now is one of maintenance. Can she sustain her massive popularity in a genre where mid-thirties is considered retirement age? Responses from several prominent music writers echo her own expressed sentiments: She can keep on rockin' for a few more years with no trouble.

DAVID REDFERN/RETNA

PHIL LOFTUS/RETNA

In 1985 at a dinner held prior to the American Music Awards

Nelson George, *Billboard*'s black music editor, while warning that "what happens down the road is dependent to a large degree on whether the movie flops and the subsequent tour is a bomb," expresses optimistic certainty: "She'll still sell quite a few records with the follow-up to *Private Dancer*. It was such a great record that it's earned her immediate airplay for whatever comes after it; Tina will maintain her status as a major celebrity for at least months into the foreseeable future."

Philadelphia Inquirer critic Ken Tucker also feels she will retain her prominence in the coming months—[as long as] she keeps making gritty dance music/uptempo type of songs. She can achieve a synthesis of sound; an updated, fresh kind of music that also has the power of the music she did with Ike."

However, *Boston Phoenix* music editor Milo Miles does sound one ominous note in his forecasts for Tina's continued success: "She has to pick and choose like white singers like Linda Ronstadt have had to do. She has to make her records very carefully. Tina can't churn out records; nor can she settle for average, mediocre material. However, she seems to understand herself pretty well, or at least she's been working lately with people who understand her well. Still I'm totally sure she could survive a bad record and hold onto her status."

When asked to give reasons for her enormous popularity, the critics all point to things already frequently cited: timeliness, her legendary background, her trials and tribulations, and the attractiveness of her image to contemporary audiences. "She filled a void in the current pop scene," Tucker said. Luckily she came along at a time when radio was just breaking down racist barriers, and a combination of her being the first really strong female voice to come along in quite a while and the fact that the songs from the *Private Dancer* album were such hits contributed to the overwhelming media attention.

Syndicated columnist, author, and critic Dave Marsh and writer/broadcaster Pablo Guzman point out that young audiences don't know much about her early days and are fascinated by her past. That has played a pivotal role. "She was a familiar face to some people and a stranger to others," says Marsh. "She had that humiliating cock-sucker microphone routine that she'd been subjected to from the old days, which in a sense is what the album (*Private Dancer*) is about, and there's the contradiction. But she's a great singer in a time

A triumphant Tina at the 1985 Grammy Awards. She won three trophies and viewed the event as the highlight of her career and vindication for the lean years she endured after leaving Ike.

ANN SUMMA/RETNA

when there are few great singers and *Private Dancer* is a great record; plus she's also an adult and it clearly shows."

"She was really raw at one time," Guzman adds. "She didn't know her instrument [voice]. Now she's got a lot more experience and it's been translated into her craft. She's moved from the B-movie level to the A-ranks. She's in the front ranks now."

Nelson George also points to the vital element of video. "In an age of video artists and a time when the video images of musicians were as important as the musicians themselves, she was already a video artist; her striking face, incredible legs and dynamic energy were tailored for video merchants.

Tina signs autographs at one of her many record store appearances to promote *Private Dancer.*

ANDREA LAUBACH/RETNA

BOB LEAFE

Tina pops up at the 1985 MTV Awards as both presenter and nominee, for "What's Love Got to Do with It."

Plus, she has a good sense of herself, and she has the mythology of the sixties and the Revue to fall back on."

No one really sees any threat to Tina's continued success from things like the South Africa issue, even though Guzman says that political questions give rise to the only problems he's had with Tina. However, the matter of audience and the composition of her fans do lead to some interesting assessments.

Nelson George not only doesn't see the legacy of the South African tour as a problem—unless anti-apartheid groups band together against her—but observes that Tina's image and appeal are being consciously tailored away from the black audience anyway. "I don't think Tina really gives that much consideration to the black audience anymore. She's more of a straight rock artist; that's who she's trying to reach, and although her albums are still selling well in the black community, that's not her prime concern."

But Guzman sees this in the context of a changing youth market, a change that Tina may have played a pivotal role in helping to usher in. "In my travels on the street I see young black kids in the same gear as the heavy metal white kids; they're listening to some of the same kinds of music and Tina's had a lot of appeal to them. The young white kids remember her from the time with the Stones and the Rod Stewart show and the Acid Queen on *Tommy*. The older black audiences—the people over thirty-five—may not be so over-

joyed at some of her statements or her image, but in the younger camp she's loved tremendously, as well as among professional white women, who see her as a role model because she's still going strong after all these years."

Tucker and Miles also cite her ability to reach the young across color lines as critical, and they don't see that waning in the next few months. Only Dave Marsh sees a possible problem with her image and audience appeal. "She wanted the high end of the crossover dream. She's not completely aware of all that entails, of all that it takes to be a successful rock star in the eighties."

While everyone feels Tina can maintain her pace, no one is certain what the next step will or should be. "Where she goes next will be very interesting," Marsh speculates. "She could make the right record commercially but the wrong record in the long run, a record that could fit into a nightclub but would be totally wrong for her. It also depends on what direction her manager wants to take her. He could take her into the same

ANN SUMMA/RETNA

Lionel Richie, with whom Tina toured in 1984, offers his congratulations at the 1985 Grammys.

kind of career as Olivia Newton-John; that would be a real safe career. On the other hand, they may want her to go more in the route of a Diana Ross or a more polished Millie Jackson. Maybe she could fill up the large arenas; that may be the best way to go."

There is unanimous agreement that her work with English musicians has been a big plus for her career, and no one seems inclined to suggest that she desert them at this point. Ken Tucker does stress his feeling that she could work easily with American composers and musicians, and he says he expects her to do so at some future date.

Ironically, when asked what one thing they felt could prove most damaging to Tina Turner, none of the critics mentioned scandal or physical infirmity. Everyone stressed a dud follow to *Private Dancer*. There's an apprehension building as the time nears for the follow. *Private Dancer*'s greatness makes us wonder if perhaps that might be for Tina and company what *The Invisible Man* was for Ralph Ellison—the giant achievement that could not be equalled or followed. However, everyone also quickly tempers their fears with the confidence that she'll be right back in the groove with the next LP.

My own feelings are that Tina Turner will continue as a major star through the eighties and that she'll make several other fine albums. I don't think she'll ever top or even necessarily equal *Private Dancer*, in part because she no longer has to make the kind of statement or bare her soul the way she had to in order to pull off that album. Not that she won't have to keep on making penetrating, personal music and hook the audience. It's just that *Private Dancer* expunged the last vestige of the Ike days and wrapped up the process of remaking Tina Turner. Interestingly, she has begun toning down her public persona at the same time that she seeks action and bawdy film roles. But then contradictions remain a major feature of her personality, so it's not surprising that she'd be deep into another one.

BARRY LEVINE

RETNA

148

All smiles, a frequent 1985 pose

I remain puzzled, impressed with, disheartened to some degree, and amazed by Tina Turner. The continual wooing of the hard-rock bunch I accept as inevitable, but I am puzzled by some of her seemingly dismissive comments regarding her musical background; the unnecessary putdowns of black music and her heritage I shrug off mentally as part of the game even as I recoil emotionally. But when "Show Some Control" comes on the radio, and her shivering, haughty, magical voice cuts through the conventional rhythm, then I am impressed—again I know what makes her the star she is. The woman is real. You can feel and hear that, and as long as that quality remains I'll forgive almost anything.

ROSS MARINO

Discography

Ike and Tina Turner Revue LPS

The best Revue albums are sadly long out of print; only scatterings of this definitive material has made its way back into circulation via auctions, collector sales, and anthologies. Consequently, if you ever spot any of the Sue albums on any record shelf, grab them immediately at whatever the cost. They are worth it.

1960–1965 (EARLY PERIOD)

The Soul of Ike and Tina Turner	Sue LP-2001 (mono)
Dance	Sue LP-2003 (mono)
Dynamite	Sue LP-2004 (mono)
Don't Play Me Cheap	Sue LP-2005 (mono)
It's Gonna Work Out Fine	Sue LP-2007 (mono)

If you don't wish to burden yourself further, these five albums will tell you all you need to know about the Revue. The *It's Gonna Work Out Fine* LP contains the single of the same title, which is often considered their best (even better than "River Deep"); but the softness of Tina's voice, the churning syncopations, and stark, aggressive sound that are conveyed through the mono tracks make these marvelous vocal documents, even if they're each weighted down in places by dreck and filler.

1965–1969 (TRANSITION/PREDISCOVERY PERIOD)

The Ike and Tina Show Live	Warner Bros. WS-1579
Revue Live	Kent 5014
The Soul of Ike and Tina Turner	Kent 5019
Festival of Live Performances	Kent 538
Show—Volume 2	Loma 5904

Confusion reigns in this period, with a wealth of recordings. Similar titles, reissues, and duplications galore make this a tough time to evaluate; the singles output towers markedly over the album releases. The Loma album is the best of a spotty bunch, with Tina doing some of her most galvanizing wailing up to this point. The Warner Bros. LP is also worth owning; the rest are now being reissued on numerous bootlegs and anthologies.

1969–1978 EVOLUTION/SPLITSVILLE

River Deep—Mountain High	Phillies; reissued on A&M in 1969
So Fine	Pompeii 6000
Cussin', Cryin' & Carryin' On	Pompeii 6004
The Hunter	Blue Thumb BTS-11
Outta Season	Blue Thumb BTS-5
In Person	Minit 24018
Come Together	Liberty LST-7637
Workin' Together	Liberty LST-7650
Her Man . . . His Woman	Capitol ST-571
Souled Out	Tangerine TRCS-1511
What You Hear Is What You Get	United Artists 2 UAS-9953
'Nuff Said	United Artists UAS-5530
Feel Good	United Artists UAS-5598
Nutbush City Limits	United Artists LA180
The Gospel According to Ike & Tina Turner	United Artists LA203
Airwaves	United Artists LA917

This period could be titled "The Rise and Fall of the Ike Empire." *River Deep* is listed here, even though it was actually recorded in 1966: It did not see the light of day in America until 1969 and was a commercial bust here, although the English loved it. It remains a controversial LP, and it is easy to view it as a failure, because Tina's voice never gets tailored, merged into, or even acclimated to the Spector wall of sound; Spector just didn't seem to understand her the way he and some critics insisted he did. Both *Cussin'* and *The Hunter* have points to recommend them; *Cussin'*, in many places, is quite prophetic, with its derived/implied scenario of couples who keep making up to break up, and *The Hunter*, with its imagery of the mercenary stalking the game is another of those cases where truth may emerge from fiction. The finest albums from this period and the ones from which you get an indication of the contemporary Tina Turner are *Come Together* and *Workin' Together*, both issued in 1970. Tina's fiery, salutory performances on the Beatles and Stones songs (e.g., the title cut and "Honky-Tonk Woman" on *Come Together;* "Get Back" and "Let It Be" on *Workin' Together*) were far more than remakes; they were cries of emancipation vocally. While the screams and blues modes are still there, we begin to get a glint of steel in the inflections, the suggestions of power that are now commonplace in her style. *Workin' Together* was an overlooked but finely done bit of social commentary as well as one of the few instances in which Ike's harmony was actually an integral part of the overall production. After the glories of these two we get a series of increasingly turgid, formalaic LPs that now tell us on vinyl what we know from other sources. Not that there aren't nuggets of good stuff on some of these. *Souled Out* reflects some of the impact of being on a Ray Charles label; Tina lets a little of the down-home side of her personality seep out occasionally. *'Nuff Said* features Tina doing more biting, caustic numbers, perhaps a response to the home situation.

Ironically, the only gold album the Revue ever garnered

came during this period. *What You Hear Is What You Get* presents the Revue at Carnegie Hall and captures their strongest, most coherent live performances before the breakup. Ike plays some blistering bass and guitar fills throughout, and Tina's whipping, churning vocals and spoken comments manage to recall, as much as any album since the Loma LP, the volatile energy the Revue created at its peak.

The final gasp came via *Nutbush City Limits,* whose title track gave them their last hit as a combined act in 1973. Tina reaches down deep to convey the wealth of emotions she feels recounting their beginnings; she's vulnerable, disgusted, weary, and weepy in alternate moments. A rather disconcerting album is *Airwaves*. Ike and Tina collaborated (to some degree) on this one in 1978, even though they had already divorced. Her career was doing zilch at the time; his wasn't setting any records either, and the reunion yielded an album that everyone is better off forgetting.

Ike and Tina Turner Revisited

Tina's present popularity has made anthologies of the old days one of the burgeoning industries on the reissue scene. Between legitimate reissues and any number of horribly dubbed and illegally released bootlegs, almost everything the group did from 1965 to the time Ike and Tina split has been recycled, and bits and pieces of the Sue days have been dispersed on foreign import anthologies. Try these, anyway.

The Greatest Hits of Ike and Tina Turner	Sue 1038
Greatest Hits	Warner Bros. WS-1810
Best	Blue Thumb BTS-49
Fantastic	Sunset 5265
Greatest Hits	Sunset 5285
Ooh Poo Pah Doo	Harmony H-30400

Something's Got a Hold on Me	Harmony H-30567
Greatest Hits	United Artists UAS-5667
World of Ike & Tina Turner	United Artists-2 LA064
Greatest Hits	United Artists LA592
16 Great Performances	ABC 4014
Too Hot to Hold	Springboard International 4011
Get It—Get It	Pickwick 3328
Workin' Together	Pickwick 3032; later reissued as 3606
Hot n' Sassy	Accord SN-7147

If this massive listing of repeated titles and reissues of reissues doesn't tell you much about many of the folks operating in the record business, nothing will. It's highly doubtful whether royalties were ever awarded as liberally as these titles got reissued and repressed. It's easy here to wind up purchasing the same record under a different title (maybe two different titles), so a word to the wise should be sufficient. If you believe that greatest hits albums serve a useful purpose, your purchase line should go something like this: the Sue (now available in German import), the Warner's, and the double-record United Artists set. If you don't have the original *Workin' Together*, spring for the remake. All the Kent albums listed in the previous section are making their way back into circulation, so grab the one titled *The Soul of Ike and Tina Turner*—it's got all the modern material on it. There's also a Kent purposely deleted here because it qualifies as a high-risk purchase. The album is titled *Please, Please, Please* and consists of a live 1970 performance. It's horribly recorded; audio levels are so bad that words get garbled routinely, and music fades up and down like a radio struggling to hold onto a distant signal. For fanatics only.

The Blue Thumb and United Artists greatest hits packages are strictly for diehard fans; the albums these songs were culled from aren't any great shakes, either. The same rings true for the ABC and Sunset material. Even if you have no feelings one way or another on the issue of bootlegs, avoid the

Springboards, Pickwicks, and Accords. While they're not really bootlegs from the standpoint of having been ripped off from tapes and churned out as eighth-generation quality dubs masquerading as records, the sound and informational shortcomings of these are such that only someone buying their first ceramic cartridge turntable should even think about wasting money on them. Sadly, these records are more widely available in major stores than almost anything else listed.

Ike and Tina Solo

This is perhaps not really a fair category; Ike's recorded moments swallow up Tina's until *Private Dancer's* release; then he becomes a footnote. Also, the truly great Ike Turner material probably won't appeal to current fans; it's right out of the classic Delta blues/rockabilly mode from which southern soul and rock and roll later emerged. It's also got deep links with country, at least in terms of sensibility.

IKE TURNER

Ike Turner Rocks the Blues	Crown CST-367
Ike Turner & the Kings of Rhythm	Flyright
Ike Turner & Kings of Rhythm	Red Lightnin'
Ike Turner—Hey Hey	Red Lightnin'-2
Black Man's Soul	Pompeii 6003
Blues Roots	United Artists UAS-5576
Confined to Soul	United Artists LA051
The Edge	Fantasy 9597 (August 1980; not to be confused with recent Tina LP of same name)

The first four albums on this list are essential to understanding how the Revue operated before Tina came in and how Ike fitted it around her. The Crown and Red Lightnin' albums feature the Delta shuffle/boogie rhythm prominently. It's a different beat from the Texas shuffle, not quite as loping and more choppy with crackling, zipping guitar licks rather than the whines and shudders of blues players like Albert Collins. The instrumentals are the real attraction on these albums. They show that Ike never really replaced Brenston as a vocalist until Tina came along. *Hey Hey* gives glimpses of soul and gospel styles in ferment as well as the ever-present blues, and spotlights the other orchestra musicians a bit more than the others, while the Flyright shows off more of Ike's arranging talents and his concept of how horns should be worked into the band.

The Pompeii album was done in 1969, and the United Artists LPs in 1972–73. The United Artists albums featured the Family Vibes as backup band. These albums don't have either the spirited interplay between Ike and Tina or the kind of steady, grinding energy that the old Kings of Rhythm had; they are unfocused, poorly produced, and half-heartedly presented and sung. *The Edge* is well titled. By 1980 Ike had seemingly lost his interest in music; he churned out tepid up-tempo pieces and hackneyed ballads that give the listener the notion that the artist is a beginner in the business or someone who's lost motivation. Ike now resides quietly in East St. Louis, having to deal with a monstrous image problem since news of the circumstances surrounding his split with Tina has appeared in magazines and newspapers across the world. The excellence contained in his earlier recordings can't erase this legacy, but they will serve to remind the world that Ike Turner accomplished some things before he met Tina and that he might have had a fine career on his own if they'd never met.

TINA TURNER

Let Me Touch Your Mind	United Artists UAS-5660
Turns the Country On	United Artists LA200
Acid Queen	LA495
The Edge (recorded in 1976, but not released until early 1985)	Fantasy
Rough	United Artists LA919
Private Dancer	Capitol ST-12330

The ultimate before-and-after process. *Private Dancer* erases, demolishes—you name it—the rest of the items listed above. As for the others, Tina clearly hasn't got a clue as to what's happening on almost every track of these solo albums. Her first solo venture, *Let Me Touch Your Mind,* is notable only for moments of such high-pitched explosion that she rivals Yoko Ono at her turned-on worst. She sounds so woeful doing country on *Turns the Country On,* you would think she grew up overseas. *Acid Queen* has moments of interest; her campy performance in the *Tommy* film ties into the overall setting of blissed-out panic. *Rough* represents the first stages toward trying to turn the image around; she sings harder and tries to convince you she's tougher, and the old Revue image of a shaking, sexy mama gets sharpened a bit. But *Private Dancer* turns the beat around (it's now clear what she was trying to do with *Rough*). The production values are remarkable, and Tina has busted out with the kind of serious rock and straight talk that she says she always wanted to do. It's probably a foregone conclusion that none of her solo albums went gold; instead, most became rust. But there's one other LP that's recently drifted across the horizon—a nifty collection of flawed items titled *The Edge*. When it was recorded, Tina was near the end physically and mentally; Fantasy Records had had this in the vault for years and should have left it there. The attempts at generating emotion and representative performance in the wake of disaster by Tina are commendable, but this is not a good or even significant album, and only those who sit up nights and count vinyl should consider getting it, even at discount prices.